COERCIVE INTERROGATION & FALSE CONVICTION

AF693404

While every precaution has been taken in the preparation of this book, the publisher assumes no responsibility for errors or omissions, or for damages resulting from the use of the information contained herein.

COERCIVE INTERROGATION & FALSE CONVICTION

First edition. December 29, 2025.

Copyright © 2025 Brian Leslie.

ISBN: 979-8233537653

Written by Brian Leslie.

Table of Contents

ABOUT THE AUTHOR

Brian Leslie is a Nationally Recognized and court qualified expert in State, Federal & Military Courts in coercive interrogation, interviews and investigative methods. Contact Brian Leslie for Free consultations at brian@criminalcaseconsultants.com . Find more about Brian Leslie by going to www.brianlesliemedia.com .

Or Call 1-888-400-1309

U.S. NATIONAL EXPERT IN:

Coerced Interrogations
Witnesses / Victim Interviews
Sexual Assault Allegations
Flawed Investigations

PROLOGUE

The Thin Line Between Truth and Deception

In the dimly lit room, the air is thick with tension. A suspect sits across from an interrogator, the weight of the situation pressing down on them. The interrogator leans in, their voice calm yet insistent, weaving a narrative that seems plausible, even inevitable. The suspect, exhausted and vulnerable, begins to question their own memory, their own truth. What follows is a confession—a moment that will change their life forever. But is it the truth, or a product of coercion? This book delves into the complex and often controversial world of interrogations and false confessions, exploring the techniques, psychology, and consequences of a system that walks a fine line between justice and injustice.

THE ART OF QUESTIONING: INTERVIEWS VS. INTERROGATIONS

The chairs are arranged in precise rows, every surface scrubbed to an institutional polish. Posters cautioning against evidence contamination line the walls of the law enforcement training classroom, their stern warnings competing with the more lurid displays of criminal timelines and mug shots. At the front, an experienced investigator stands at ease, blazer unbuttoned, posture radiating the confidence of someone who has long since mastered the routine of command.

On the whiteboard behind him, two columns are labeled in block letters: INTERVIEW on the left, INTERROGATION on the right. Between them, a thick vertical line underscores the promise of clarity. The investigator—his hair graying at the temples, eyes sharp and direct—waits for the last of the attendees to settle before speaking.

"Let's begin with the fundamentals," he says, voice pitched to reach the back of the room without strain. "Interview versus interrogation. Two techniques, two distinct outcomes."

He gestures to the left column. "Interview: non-accusatory, open-ended, a process of gathering information. In an interview, you treat the subject as a witness—someone who might have insight, not necessarily involvement."

The instructor pauses, letting his gaze roam over the trainees. Most are in uniform, but a handful wear plainclothes, marked out by their lack of insignia. All are rapt, pens hovering above notepads.

"Now—interrogation." He taps the right column with a marker. "Accusatory. Confession-focused. Here, the subject isn't just someone with information—they are the source, the problem, the puzzle to be solved." He clicks the cap back on the marker and turns, hands clasped behind his back. "The psychological difference, ladies and gentlemen, is night and day. If you don't recognize when you've crossed that line, you might as well hand your case to the defense right now."

A ripple of nervous laughter. The investigator smiles, a brief flash of amusement that never reaches his eyes.

He steps away from the whiteboard, approaching a row of desks. "Consider your posture in an interview. Open, receptive, mirroring the body language of your subject." He gestures for a volunteer and a young woman, all sharp edges and high cheekbones, stands and joins him at the front. He motions to a pair of chairs positioned in a gentle angle, rather than directly across from one another.

"Notice the arrangement," he says, lowering himself into one chair while the volunteer sits in the other. "I'm not looming, not threatening. My hands are visible, my body language relaxed." He leans back, ankles crossed, and smiles at his counterpart. "The message is clear: we're equals. I'm here to listen."

He swivels to the class. "Compare that to the setup in an interrogation." Without prompting, he brings both chairs to face each other squarely, the distance between them shrinking until knees almost touch. The smile fades. His posture straightens, hands folded on the table. The transformation is subtle but absolute: authority is asserted, the pressure is tangible.

"In this configuration, control is everything. You establish dominance, you direct the flow. The subject feels it, even if they're not consciously aware." He holds the gaze of the volunteer for a beat longer than is comfortable. She blinks, glancing away first.

"Thank you," he says, and the woman returns to her seat, face flushed.

He addresses the trainees. "Your environment amplifies these effects. A comfortable room with a window? That's for interviews. Four blank walls and a bolted-down chair? That's an interrogation suite."

He paces before the whiteboard, warming to the topic. "Let's go deeper. What about your questions?" He uncaps the marker, draws an arrow under INTERVIEW. "Start with open-ended inquiries. Tell me what happened. Walk me through the night. Let the subject guide the narrative." Under INTERROGATION, he writes: "Direct, confrontational. You know why you're here. Explain these inconsistencies."

He stops and faces the class, arms folded. "The transition point—the moment you shift from interview to interrogation—is pivotal. Mishandle it, and you might lose your subject's trust, or worse, your legal standing. The key is intent: when you believe, based on evidence or intuition, that this person isn't just a witness but your suspect, everything changes. Your language, your tone, even how you arrange the chairs."

A hand rises near the back of the room. The investigator nods in acknowledgment.

"Sir, what about cases where the subject doesn't realize they've become a suspect? Do you maintain the interview posture?"

He grins. "Excellent question. Sometimes, you want them comfortable, unsuspecting. Sometimes, you let the suspicion hang in the air and watch how they squirm. But once you go accusatory, there's no going back. You can't un-ring that bell." He uncaps the marker and writes on the bottom of the board: "No return to rapport once it's broken."

He claps his hands once. "Let's do an exercise." The room shifts, a collective straightening. "Pair up. One of you is the interviewer, the other the subject. Your goal: establish whether this person was at the scene of a crime. First round, use interview techniques. Second round, switch to interrogation."

The room erupts in a low hum as trainees pivot in their seats, some exchanging nervous glances. The investigator circulates, offering commentary. "Use open posture. Empathize. Mirror their language." At another pair: "Now, lean in. Lower your voice. Pin them to a detail and don't let go."

He halts beside a young man who towers over his partner, arms crossed. "Relax," the instructor says. "You're not intimidating a confession out of a vending machine." The man chuckles, uncrossing his arms, and the atmosphere lightens.

After several minutes, he calls for attention. "What did you notice?" Silence, then a tentative voice: "Subjects volunteered more information when we stayed friendly." Nods around the room.

"And during interrogation?"

A different trainee: "People got defensive. Sometimes they clammed up."

"Exactly." The investigator nods. "Human nature. You escalate too quickly, they shut down. You stay too soft, and you might miss a confession. The art," he says, voice dropping, "is in knowing where to draw the line, and when."

He returns to the front of the room, resting a hand on the whiteboard. "Here's a rule of thumb: treat everyone like a witness until you can't. Once suspicion hardens, move deliberately. No one ever confessed because they were shouted into submission. Confessions happen when people feel it's their only option."

A murmur of assent ripples through the room.

He checks his watch, then delivers the final point. "Remember: The moment you decide someone is a suspect rather than a witness, everything changes—your questions, your tone, even how you arrange the chairs. Get that wrong, and the whole case can unravel."

He wipes the board clean with a practiced sweep, then gestures for the class to stand.

"Break. Fifteen minutes. When we return, we'll discuss the psychological impact of these techniques."

The room empties in a scatter of footsteps and whispered debriefs, but the words linger, etched into the blank expanse of the whiteboard and the collective memory of the future investigators.

The training resumes not in the familiar classroom, but in an amphitheater bristling with AV equipment and the scent of fresh coffee. The atmosphere has shifted: the rigid authority of law enforcement now tempered by the clinical calm of academic psychology. Onstage, a woman in a tailored navy suit arranges her notes with surgical precision, her every movement deliberate, as if efficiency itself were a core principle.

Behind her, an enormous projection screen displays a cross-section of the human brain, its circuitry lit in colors that oscillate with each click of the remote. The audience—a mixture of police, detectives, and visiting legal professionals—leans forward, awaiting the translation of their fieldwork into the language of neural impulses.

"Thank you for the introduction," she begins, her voice modulated to soothe and instruct. "What we're going to examine today is the mental and emotional toll exacted by different methods of questioning—how your approach as investigators quite literally alters the brain chemistry of your subjects."

She taps the remote and the slide changes: two superimposed brain scans, one blue and calm, the other pulsing red along the amygdala. "This is a scan of a subject during a neutral interview," she says, pointing to the tranquil image. "Notice the distributed, balanced activity. Now, compare to this scan, taken during a high-pressure interrogation. See the intense activity here, and here? That's the stress response. The body is reacting as if to a physical threat."

Murmurs ripple through the audience. A few trainees scribble notes with fresh urgency.

She paces slowly, letting the science settle. "Why does this matter? Because stress isn't just an unpleasant feeling—it fundamentally changes how we process questions, recall memories, and make decisions. Under extreme stress, the brain releases cortisol and adrenaline, priming the subject for fight, flight, or—" she pauses, leveling a finger for emphasis "—freeze. Which, as you know, can manifest as silence or apparent stubbornness in the interrogation room."

She advances the slide. Now, two video windows play side by side. On the left: a man in his mid-thirties, clean-cut, hands folded in his lap, calmly responding to questions from an unseen interviewer. On the right: another subject, similar age, but sweating visibly under the collar, fingers drumming a relentless tattoo on the tabletop.

"In interviews," the expert narrates, "the subject's parasympathetic nervous system remains engaged. This allows for trust, rapport, and truthful disclosure." She gestures to the calm man, who volunteers information with slow, measured speech.

"But during an interrogation," she says, voice tightening, "sympathetic arousal takes over. Heart rate rises, pupils dilate, body language betrays a defensive posture." The second video shows the sweating man, who shrinks into his seat as the questioner's tone grows sharper. When pressed, his answers become clipped, evasive; at several points, he visibly hesitates, glancing down and away.

"These aren't just quirks of personality," the expert continues. "They are physiological facts. You can see them—hear them—in the timbre of a suspect's voice, in the micro-movements of their eyes and hands. The stress response is not voluntary."

A hand goes up in the audience. The expert nods.

"Isn't some stress useful? Don't people sometimes confess when they feel pressure?"

She smiles, appreciative but unyielding. "Pressure can work. But it's a double-edged sword. Push too hard, and the subject's cognitive resources are depleted. They become less capable of distinguishing truth from suggestion, more prone to say what they think you want to hear. That's how you get false confessions, or bad intel."

She clicks to a new slide: a line graph charting cognitive endurance over time. "Interviews, even lengthy ones, have a relatively stable pattern—subjects remain oriented and coherent. But interrogations show a steep drop-off after the first hour. Attention falters. Memory distorts. Anxiety hijacks the narrative, and by the end, subjects may confess to actions they didn't commit just to escape the stressor."

She lets the silence stretch, the gravity of the data landing with a palpable weight.

"Consider this in your fieldwork," the expert concludes, scanning the room. "A suspect who recants, or whose story changes drastically over time, isn't necessarily lying. They may simply be suffering the neurological consequences of high-pressure tactics. As investigators, your responsibility isn't just to get answers—it's to know which answers are real."

She kills the projection, leaving the brain scans lingering in afterimage. "Any questions?"

An older detective raises his hand, voice hoarse from years of cigarettes. "How do you tell the difference, then, between someone breaking under pressure and someone who's just guilty?"

The expert steps closer, folding her arms. "Look for the consistency of detail, not just emotional display. A guilty subject often tries to manage their impression, but their story holds together under gentle pressure. A stressed but innocent subject will flounder, contradict themselves, or go blank—not out of malice, but because their memory is short-circuited by anxiety."

A nod, slow and thoughtful.

She dismisses the group with a final, measured note: "Remember: prolonged stress is a confounder, not a shortcut. The most reliable confessions come from the clearest minds, not the most battered ones."

As the attendees shuffle out, the images of frantic, glowing brains and sweat-stained interviews follow them, lingering reminders of the invisible forces at play behind every closed door.

Morning in the precinct brings a bleary-eyed gravity distinct from the ordered tension of the classroom or the clinical chill of the lecture hall. Coffee in hand, officers shuffle into the briefing room, the worn conference table scarred with decades of departmental history. The mood is subdued, but alert; the promise of actionable information hovers, unspoken, over every seat.

At the head of the table stands a senior detective, forty years in the service and it shows in the deep creases at the eyes and the map of pale scars on the hands. The detective's manner is clipped, but never hurried, as if each word had been measured, weighed, and then spoken only if necessary.

A laptop projects onto a battered screen at the far end, displaying a bold header: DECISION MATRIX – INTERVIEW VS INTERROGATION. Beneath it, a three-column checklist gleams against the institutional beige of the wall.

"Settle in," the detective says, voice low but carrying. "Today we're going to talk about choosing the right approach. Not just for your cases, but for your careers."

The first item appears onscreen: BEHAVIORAL CUES.

"We all know the basics," the detective begins, laser pointer steady in hand. "Avoiding eye contact, inconsistent stories, defensive posture. But the devil's in the details." The pointer circles a bulleted list. "Take 'avoiding eye contact.' Sometimes it's a tell for lying, sure. But in other cultures, or with anxious types, it's a sign of respect or discomfort—not deceit."

A hand shoots up. The detective nods.

"What if you're not sure which it is?"

The detective grins, a flash of gold crown. "You never are, one hundred percent. That's why you use clusters. If you see three or four tells together—hesitation, deflection, closed body language—you start to build a pattern. But never hang your hat on one indicator. Ever."

Next: EVIDENCE STRENGTH.

The screen transitions to a split display: CIRCUMSTANTIAL on the left, DIRECT on the right. "Here's where people get tripped up," the detective says, pacing in a tight, predatory arc. "You may have a hunch—a strong one. But if all you have is circumstantial, tread carefully. Push too hard, and the defense will eat you alive. Wait until you have at least some direct evidence before you turn up the heat in interrogation."

A ripple of acknowledgment through the room. The senior detective continues.

"Which brings us to SUSPECT PROFILE." A new list appears: prior criminal history, proximity to victim, recent life stressors. "No two suspects are the same. Some cave after a single accusatory question; others, you couldn't break with a sledgehammer." A muted chuckle from the back row.

"But here's the trick," the detective says, holding up a finger. "Guilty people practice. Innocent people don't. A guilty suspect might meet your gaze too readily, have their story rehearsed down to the syllable. An innocent party often falters, gets details out of order, seems...less polished. That doesn't mean they're lying—it means they haven't thought about being accused."

A young officer in the second row leans forward. "What about stress reactions? Sometimes people get so nervous they just start sweating, or laughing, or even crying. Doesn't mean they're guilty, right?"

The detective nods. "Correct. Nervous doesn't equal guilty. What you're looking for is the why. If someone starts perspiring when you mention a time or a place, note it. If they're nervous the entire time, could be the setting. Could be you." The detective lets that last bit hang, a silent challenge.

A few of the officers scribble reminders in their notebooks, circling points for later.

The presentation moves to CASE EXAMPLES. The screen flashes images: an older man gripping his chair with white-knuckle tension; a teenage girl with arms crossed so tightly it looks painful; a woman whose hands flutter ceaselessly above the table, never settling.

The detective narrates. "First case, the old man. Wouldn't meet our eyes, stuttered when pressed on timelines. Turned out he'd had a minor stroke six months prior, and his recall was compromised. Not deception—neurology."

Next image. "Teenager. Clammed up every time we asked about her whereabouts. Turns out, she'd been skipping school and didn't want her parents to know, but she wasn't connected to the crime at all."

Last: "The woman with the nervous hands. She broke down in the second hour and confessed to a fraud scheme that wasn't even on our radar. Point is: you need to tune your approach, not just for the case, but for the individual."

The checklist shifts to the final item: TIMING AND ESCALATION.

"Jumping to interrogation too quickly can shut down a cooperative witness, while interviewing a guilty suspect too gently might let them craft a better lie." The detective scans the room, making sure the point sticks. "You only get one clean shot at the initial statement. Don't waste it."

A final, practical note. "If you're ever in doubt, do a soft interview first. Let them get comfortable. Let them underestimate you. If you're still suspicious after, escalate—but only with purpose. Don't play all your cards at once."

The screen fades to black, replaced by the station's weathered crest. The detective's eyes sweep the table, challenging anyone to contradict or question.

"Questions?"

Silence, but for the shuffling of paper.

"Good," the detective says. "Because if you screw this up, the case is toast, and so is your reputation. Treat every interview and every interrogation like your badge depends on it. It probably does."

The session breaks. Officers spill into the hallway, checklist fresh in their minds, the boundary between interview and interrogation now both clearer and more fraught.

The final session of the training is held not in a classroom, but in a makeshift courtroom, complete with wood paneling and the austere dignity of due process. The arrangement is deliberate—each decision, each line of questioning, is about to be put on trial.

At the bench sits a panel of legal experts: a retired judge, two criminal defense attorneys, and the program's lead instructor. Before them, the audience—investigators, police, and a smattering of students—arrange themselves in ascending rows, prepared to watch real-world consequences unfold in meticulous detail.

The lead instructor opens the session. "Today, we'll examine three case studies where the distinction between interview and interrogation was blurred or ignored—with disastrous results. Each is a matter of public record, and each underscores the gravity of our work."

A click, and the first case appears onscreen. A file photo of a teenager, unremarkable except for the haunted look in his eyes.

"Case One," the instructor says, "State v. Pegram. The subject: a sixteen-year-old with mild cognitive delays. The event: a convenience store robbery. No priors, no history of violence."

The instructor's tone is measured, but there's an undercurrent of barely masked anger. "During the investigation, the subject was placed in an interrogation suite for nine hours. No guardian, no advocate, no break. For the first three hours, the questioning was interview-style: open, neutral. By hour four, the technique shifted—rapidly—into accusatory, even confrontational. They told him there was security footage—there wasn't. They implied his friends had already confessed—they hadn't."

A transcript excerpt fills the screen:

INVESTIGATOR: "We know you did it. If you admit it now, the judge will go easy."

SUSPECT: "I didn't, but—can I go home if I say I did?"

The instructor lets the words hang for a moment before continuing.

"After nine hours, the subject gave a detailed confession. It contradicted known facts and contained errors only a non-witness would make. It took forensic analysis and outside advocacy to reverse the conviction. But the cost—years lost, trust shattered—cannot be undone."

A defense attorney on the panel interjects, "This is a classic failure of age-appropriate interviewing. Juveniles—especially those with cognitive delays—are highly susceptible to suggestion and coercion. The move to aggressive interrogation should never have happened."

The instructor nods, face set. "A reminder: treat vulnerability with heightened care. You cannot interrogate a confession out of a child, only out of your own conscience."

The slide shifts to the next case. This time, a middle-aged man in a business suit, his expression blank with fatigue.

"Case Two. City v. Sanchez. The subject: a bank manager, witness to an armed robbery. He provided an initial statement, but inconsistencies led investigators to suspect involvement."

A timeline appears:

- Initial interview: non-accusatory, rapport-based.

- Follow-up interview: rapidly escalates to accusatory.

- Subject ceases cooperation after being accused.

The instructor gestures to the table. "What happened here? After the first session, the witness was willing—eager, even—to help. But at the first hint of suspicion, the interviewer went full interrogation, switching tone, language, and posture. The witness immediately clammed up, lawyered up, and refused to provide further information."

The retired judge weighs in. "A premature shift to interrogation is a tactical blunder. You lose your most cooperative witness and gain nothing in return. It's not just a legal issue—it's an operational failure."

The instructor calls up an excerpt from the internal review:

INVESTIGATOR: "Your story doesn't add up, Mr. Sanchez."

WITNESS: "So I'm a suspect now?"

INVESTIGATOR: "If you've got nothing to hide, why are you getting upset?"

"Classic mistake," the instructor says. "They assumed that defensiveness equaled guilt, not realizing that shock and fear can provoke the same reaction in an innocent person. The case ultimately stalled. The real perpetrator was caught months later, by pure coincidence."

Murmurs ripple through the gallery. The instructor's face darkens as the third case is displayed.

"Case Three. People v. Wei. Here, cultural misinterpretation led to a catastrophic error. The subject, a recent immigrant, was questioned as a witness to an assault. The interviewer noticed that she never made eye contact, answered in brief, hesitant phrases, and kept her hands folded in her lap."

The instructor's eyes scan the audience. "The investigator read these as classic signs of deception. The reality: in her culture, direct eye contact is a sign of disrespect, and deference is expected when speaking to authority."

The transcript is brutal in its clarity:

INVESTIGATOR: "Why are you so nervous, Ms. Wei?"

WITNESS: "I am not nervous. I want to help."

INVESTIGATOR: "You're acting like you have something to hide."

The instructor turns from the screen, tone colder. "As a result, the witness was treated as a suspect. The real witness statements were discounted, and the trail went cold for weeks. Only after a cultural liaison intervened was the mistake corrected—but the damage to trust was permanent."

The judge on the panel addresses the room. "These aren't just errors. They're miscarriages of justice—each the result of failing to distinguish between interview and interrogation, and of misreading the human being across the table."

The instructor stands, arms folded. "Remember what's at stake. Every decision you make—every word, every question—ripples outward. You are not just seeking truth; you are shaping it, for better or for worse."

A hush settles as the presentation ends.

The instructor delivers the closing argument. "The choice between interview and interrogation isn't just procedural—it can determine whether justice is served, or denied. Never forget that the person in that chair, guilty or not, deserves the benefit of your best judgment."

The session is dismissed. As the crowd files out—quiet, thoughtful, some visibly shaken—the lessons of the day linger, solemn as a verdict.

THE ANATOMY OF AN INTERROGATION ROOM

The hallway leading to the interrogation suite is featureless and silent, lined with acoustic tile that deadens both footsteps and conversation. Security cameras sit in each corner, their red lights winking at every passerby. An unmarked metal door—dented, the paint chipped from years of use—guards the entrance. It can only be unlocked from the outside.

Inside: sensory deprivation. The walls are blocky, painted in a shade between eggshell and surgical gray, interrupted only by the hairline cracks where drywall meets concrete. No posters, no instructional slogans, no last vestige of personality. Overhead, fluorescent tubes flicker in and out of phase with a faint, persistent hum—light that bathes everything in a low-resolution blue-white.

The first thing to catch the eye is the table. Rectangular, utilitarian, steel legs welded to a plate that's bolted directly to the floor. Its surface is scrubbed clean, save for the occasional scuff mark or gouge where previous participants—nervous, angry, or desperate—have dug in their nails. There is no give in the table. It is both boundary and anchor, dividing the room as surely as any physical barrier could.

Opposite the entrance, two chairs: one for the interrogator, one for the suspect. They are not equal. The interrogator's chair is slightly taller, with a high back and padded seat. It features armrests, which allow the user to relax, to dominate with casual authority, to lean in or recline at will. The suspect's chair, by contrast, is the bare minimum of comfort: molded plastic, legs too short, seat sloping backward just enough to put the occupant at a constant disadvantage. There are no armrests. It is always placed with its back to the door, ensuring the suspect cannot see who might enter next, or when. The legs are often equipped with silent rubber pads, preventing the chair from being shifted out of alignment or weaponized in a moment of panic.

There are rarely windows, and if present, they are defensive—small, high on the wall, with frosted glass that distorts all shapes behind it. The only exception is the observation mirror. Installed at eye level and stretching nearly the width of the wall, it's a one-way sheet that allows witnesses, superiors, or legal counsel to observe without being observed. Suspects know instinctively that they are watched, but never by whom. The glass is always cold to the touch, and rumors circulate about how it magnifies every sound made in the room.

There are no clocks. This is by design. The absence of time cues disorients even the most robust subjects, encouraging a sense of timelessness that breaks down psychological defenses. No one who has spent more than an hour here can ever say with certainty how long they have been inside.

The only decorative element, if it can be called that, is the tiled floor. Some rooms feature stark checkerboard, a visual motif that suggests both order and punishment. Others opt for muted linoleum that shows stains as a warning. Every surface is wipeable, every corner visible. Nothing is left to chance, nothing to privacy.

No personal items, no comfort objects, not even a forgotten pen. Even the air is regulated: filtered through ductwork that cycles every twelve minutes, maintaining a temperature just below what most would consider comfortable. The slight chill is constant, and it keeps everyone—suspect and interrogator alike—on edge.

There is a phone, but it does not ring. There is a camera, always on, its lens picking up every microexpression, every bead of sweat, every nervous twitch. The recording light never blinks; it merely stares.

Each design choice is intentional, a product of decades of research and thousands of hours spent watching people unravel. The sterility of the room does more than deny comfort: it denies context, hope, and sometimes, even memory. The walls, the table, the chair—all tools in a process engineered to reduce the subject to a single fact: they are not in control.

To an outsider, the room is dull, forgettable, even brutal in its sameness. To those who pass through, it becomes unforgettable, a place where time folds in on itself and the world outside stops mattering. The only way out is through, and the room is built to remind you of that, every second that passes, even if you cannot see the seconds tick by.

At the end of the walkthrough, one is left with the sense of a stage set for the purest contest of will. The room is not a place, but a condition: neutral, implacable, inescapable.

The interrogation room is only the start. What matters more than the four walls is how they are used: the active shaping of discomfort, the steady escalation of pressure until the air itself becomes suspect.

A subject is brought in, not handcuffed, but with wrists held tight in nervous anticipation. The detective's hand never leaves the man's elbow until he is deposited into the lower, plastic chair, back to the door. Before the interview even begins, two things have been established: entry is not by choice, and exit is not imminent.

Temperature is the first, subtlest lever. The climate control is set just a few degrees below comfort. This is not enough to make the teeth chatter, but enough that, after ten minutes, the skin goosebumps, and the muscles along the arms and jaw begin to tighten. Occasionally, for emphasis, the thermostat is nudged higher—just enough to produce sweat at the hairline, to smudge confidence into a sheen of humiliation. The interrogator remains immune, dressed in a suit or department-issue pullover, never betraying discomfort. Their comfort is the baseline; the suspect's, the deviation.

Lighting comes next. The overhead tubes are calibrated to a frequency that is barely perceptible but cumulative in effect. At first, the flicker registers only as an afterimage at the edge of vision. After an hour, it becomes a pulse; after two, it is an irritant, impossible to ignore. Sometimes, the interrogator will dim the lights during a pause in questioning, as if to offer relief—only to snap them back to full intensity at a critical moment, regaining the advantage. Occasionally, a desk lamp is introduced: its circle of yellow light corrals the suspect, shrinking their universe to the tabletop and whatever evidence is laid out before them.

Sound is the most versatile weapon. The room itself is muffled, but the silence is absolute. Each cough, each shuffle, each sigh echoes off the walls. This makes every spoken word heavy, every pause a chasm. Some detectives favor slow, deliberate silence, letting it fill the gaps between questions until the urge to answer becomes overwhelming. Others introduce noise by increments: the tap of a pen, the scrape of a chair, the deliberate flipping of a file page. In older stations, the hum of the HVAC system will periodically spike, rattling the ductwork like distant thunder, always unexpected and always at a moment when the suspect is trying to gather their thoughts.

Occasionally, a clock is introduced—a cheap digital model placed on the table for effect. It never shows the actual time, but cycles at random intervals, designed to disorient rather than orient. Some interrogators prefer to bring in a ticking analog clock, the rhythmic click marking time as it drains away, each second a needle in the suspect's patience.

Physical positioning is the most overt instrument of control. The detective does not sit down at once. Instead, they pace the perimeter, occasionally standing just behind the suspect's shoulder, or leaning against the wall with arms crossed. When they finally take their seat, it is always after the suspect has been left to stew alone, the weight of the room doing its work. The interrogator's chair is slightly higher, so even when seated they look down upon their subject. If the suspect slumps, the gap widens.

Proximity is manipulated with surgical precision. The detective will lean in, elbows on table, reducing the distance to less than a foot, forcing the suspect to hold eye contact or look away in defeat. At strategic moments, the detective will retreat, sitting back with a look of disappointed detachment, making the suspect chase their approval, even as they dread their judgment. On rare occasions, the interrogator circles the table entirely, appearing first at the subject's right, then left, their shadow stretching across the table as they move.

Throughout, every reaction is noted: the beads of sweat that form at the temples, the twitch of a leg under the table, the way hands clench into fists or fidget with invisible debris. Some suspects become hyperverbal, talking to fill the void left by the silence; others retreat into themselves, staring at the floor or wall, seeking a comfort that is never given. Interrogators are trained to recognize these responses, to amplify them with subtle cues—sliding a tissue box just out of reach, pausing at the door as if to leave, only to return with renewed intensity.

It is not always a contest of strength. Sometimes, the room is made softer, the light dimmed, the tone gentle, to lull the subject into a false sense of security. But the tools are always the same, and the goal never varies: the gradual erosion of resistance until confession, or collapse, is the path of least pain.

By the time the suspect is escorted out—sometimes after a half hour, sometimes after eight—every sensory channel has been worked, every axis of control exploited. The physical toll is obvious in the way they rise, stretching cramped muscles and blinking at the sudden freedom of the hallway. The psychological toll lingers, an afterimage that follows them out of the building and into the rest of their life.

For the detective, the room resets with the next entry. But for the suspect, its effects are cumulative, the discomforts and disorientations stacking one atop the other until the memory of the place is inseparable from the memory of the event itself.

The true power of the interrogation room is psychological, not physical. It is a crucible: designed to apply precise pressures, to isolate and render pliable even the most resistant personalities. Over years of use, certain effects have become so predictable that they might as well be listed in the operator's manual.

Spatial confinement is the first and most obvious effect. Even a large interrogation room feels small after an hour, the walls looming closer with each circuit the subject makes in their head. Suspects pace if allowed, but eventually, they sit—either from fatigue or because the chair is their only option for relief. The lack of windows or external reference points amplifies the sense of being trapped, a sensation that is both physical and existential. For those already prone to claustrophobia, panic attacks are common: shallow breathing, rapid heartbeat, the onset of a cold sweat that soaks through shirt and undershirt before the first substantive question is even asked.

Sensory deprivation is more insidious. The blankness of the walls, the lack of movement or color, acts as a cognitive dampener. Memory recall becomes harder, not easier; the mind, denied stimulation, turns inward and often collapses in on itself. Suspects begin to second-guess their own memories, to question the order of events, to fill gaps with whatever suggestions are offered by the interrogator. This is not a flaw, but a feature. Studies show that in such environments, compliance with authority figures increases, even as confidence in one's own recollection wanes. The effect is most pronounced in those with preexisting mental health issues, the young, or the elderly.

Time distortion is perhaps the most effective weapon. Without a clock, and with the room's artificial lighting maintaining a perpetual, unchanging brightness, time ceases to exist in the way most understand it. Subjects consistently underestimate how long they've been in the room by hours. Interrogations that last four or six hours are remembered as two or less. This temporal fog breeds exhaustion, and with exhaustion comes acquiescence. Eventually, resistance doesn't feel like an option. It doesn't even feel like a decision.

The institutional sterility of the environment compounds the effect. Every interaction, every word, is framed by the knowledge that this is not a place for negotiation. The subtext of the design is plain: the room, and by extension the institution it represents, cannot be moved. Only the person inside it can change. For some, this breeds a perverse comfort, a surrender to inevitability. For others, it leads to outbursts: tears, rage, the sudden urge to confess even to acts never committed, simply to regain some measure of agency over the situation.

Empirical studies bear this out. In one meta-analysis of over two thousand interrogation transcripts, false confessions were disproportionately associated with rooms employing the most aggressive environmental controls: low temperatures, high-wattage lighting, and complete lack of temporal orientation. In experimental simulations, subjects subjected to similar conditions became more suggestible after just ninety minutes. Their rate of error in recalling details tripled compared to those interviewed in standard office settings.

The impact is magnified in vulnerable populations. Juveniles, lacking both experience and the cognitive fortitude of adults, often break first. Their confessions are more likely to include details fed to them by investigators. The mentally ill or cognitively impaired become disoriented faster, sometimes unable to differentiate between reality and suggestion after prolonged isolation. Even the physically healthy can be broken down if the session is long enough, the environment tuned precisely to their weaknesses.

Some agencies have gone so far as to tailor room conditions to the subject. For those with known anxiety disorders, the temperature is dropped lower; for suspected sociopaths, the lighting is made even more aggressive, the interrogator's posture more dominating. There is a logic to it, but also a cruelty: a recognition that the human mind is, ultimately, just another object to be manipulated.

The ethical debate is ongoing. Some argue that these techniques are necessary, that the guilty must be made to talk by any means. Others point to the mounting body of evidence that shows such conditions not only break the guilty, but also manufacture confessions from the innocent and traumatize the already fragile.

The room, in the end, does not care. It serves its purpose, indifferent to the outcome, cycling through subject after subject with the same sterile efficiency. What is left behind, in the minds of those who pass through, is not so easily erased.

Not all interrogation rooms are relics. In recent years, some agencies have begun to experiment with "soft" interview environments—spaces that upend every expectation drilled into generations of law enforcement. The logic is not humanitarian, but evidentiary: when the room becomes less adversarial, the subject talks more, and what they say is more likely to hold up under scrutiny.

A soft interview room, at first glance, resembles a psychiatrist's office or a waiting room in a suburban dental practice. The chairs are upholstered in neutral earth tones, wide enough to sit cross-legged or to lean back without immediate discomfort. The walls are painted a shade lighter than the sky, neither sterile nor suffocating. There is art, but it is abstract—nothing that might suggest judgment or narrative. The table is circular, its edges rounded, denying both interrogator and subject the advantage of corners. If there is a window, it looks out onto a nondescript courtyard or is fitted with blinds that can be adjusted from inside.

The technology is everywhere, but almost invisible. Cameras are embedded in smoke detectors or ceiling tiles, their lenses concealed behind matte glass. Microphones are omnidirectional and noise-cancelling, able to pick up a whisper but filtering out the hum of climate control. Temperature and light are modulated by a central panel—touch a button, and the room warms, cools, brightens, or dims according to the psychological profile of the person inside.

One-way mirrors are being phased out. In their place: discreet two-way communication systems, where observers can text or ping the interviewer with real-time suggestions. This allows supervisors or psychologists to influence the process without the subject ever feeling the oppressive gaze from the other side of the glass. In some rooms, hidden speakers allow the interviewer to play calming music at just above the threshold of awareness, proven to lower heart rate and stress hormones in susceptible populations.

Instead of deprivation, there is careful stimulation. A bowl of candy on the table, sometimes a pitcher of filtered water with actual glasses. Even the presence of a tissue box serves a dual purpose: comfort for the subject, and an easy tell for the interviewer—those who reach for it are almost always more vulnerable to suggestion.

The script has changed, too. Interrogators are trained to begin each session by asking about comfort, offering a beverage, adjusting the room if requested. This is not kindness for its own sake. The goal is to lower defenses, to create a sense of agency in the subject, so that when the pressure is eventually applied, it feels like a conversation rather than an inquisition.

The results are not anecdotal. In pilot programs, confession rates remain high, but the rate of proven false confessions drops by as much as a third. Subjects interviewed in soft rooms report lower levels of post-event trauma, and more of them are willing to return voluntarily for follow-up questioning. Juveniles and the mentally ill are especially susceptible to this change—less likely to recant, more likely to tell the same story twice in a row, even when no one is watching.

Still, not all is utopian. There are those who argue that the soft room is just as manipulative as the hard one, its coercion wrapped in a veneer of comfort. The same tools are in play, merely repurposed: ambient noise replaces silence, warmth replaces cold, the illusion of choice replaces its absence. Some suspects, confronted with the incongruity between the room's appearance and their own predicament, become even more disoriented—unsure whether to trust or resist, caught between the old script and the new.

The shift is gradual. In some cities, only high-profile cases or first-time offenders are ushered into the soft rooms; in others, the change is universal, every interview now conducted in the same hushed, padded space. The old hard rooms persist, relegated to the wings of precincts or held in reserve for "special cases"—repeat offenders, violent criminals, those whom the system deems less deserving of comfort.

Every change comes with a lesson. The rooms are not just about extracting information, but about creating a record that will withstand the scrutiny of courtrooms, media, and public opinion. Soft rooms leave fewer visible scars, but the pressure to confess is still omnipresent—now delivered in a voice that is softer, a hand that is steadier, but no less insistent.

There are some who leave the new rooms feeling, if not vindicated, then at least unbroken. Others find the experience more insidious, the memory of being manipulated under the guise of comfort sticking longer than the old anxieties. For the designers of such spaces, the goal remains unchanged: to break down resistance, to secure the truth, or failing that, to secure a narrative that will hold up to the daylight outside.

The room adapts. The people inside, not always as quickly.

But the effect, as ever, is cumulative—another set of memories, another increment of pressure, recorded and replayed long after the subject has left and the room resets itself, waiting for the next.

COERCIVE TECHNIQUES: THE SLIPPERY SLOPE

The interrogation suite has been reset to its default: table perfectly centered, chairs equidistant, all evidence of prior occupation erased by a chemical tang in the air. Under the floodlights, even the seams in the linoleum gleam. The only movement is the suspect's nervous shifting in the ill-fitting plastic chair, hands twisting in his lap as if hoping friction might erase them entirely. He is pale, puffy-eyed, and draped in a t-shirt gone gray at the collar. His shoes are missing—standard precaution, but also a low-level humiliation, a reminder of dependency.

Across the table, the interrogator projects a calculated ease. The effect is studied—jacket off, sleeves rolled, tie loosened but not removed. He sits at an angle, one hip perched on the edge of the chair, posture open but canted forward just enough to signal engagement. His hands are visible at all times, resting palms-up on the tabletop, sometimes idly twiddling a capped pen. Where the suspect shrinks, the interrogator expands to fill the space, but never aggressively.

The first volley is not a question. It's a statement, delivered in a register just above a whisper: "Rough night, huh?" He doesn't wait for a response. "Those holding benches are brutal. Sorry we had to keep you in the tank so long." He lets it hang, a thin veneer of empathy layered over protocol.

The suspect blinks hard, tries to focus. "Can I just—can I call my mom?"

The interrogator smiles—sad, knowing, almost paternal. "You will. I promise. But you know how this goes. We gotta do the paperwork first. Get the story straight." He leans in, voice confidential. "Look, nobody wants to be here any longer than we have to be. Least of all me."

The dance continues. The interrogator slides a manila folder between them—nothing inside, just a prop, but the suspect doesn't know that. He taps it twice with the pen, then rests his chin on his hand. "I've been doing this a long time," he says. "And I can tell when someone's just caught up in a situation. Happens every day. Good people, bad luck."

The suspect's shoulders ease, fractionally. He looks up, meets the other's eyes for a second before looking down again.

"We know what happened wasn't really your fault," the interrogator continues, softly but with a touch of rehearsed finality. "Anyone would have reacted the same way, in your shoes. Heck, I might've, too."

This is the opening move of minimization: recast the transgression as not only understandable, but practically inevitable. Guilt is not denied, but reframed as a technicality—a small aberration in an otherwise upstanding life. The interrogator employs it with the grace of a surgeon, splitting the difference between moral censure and moral rescue. By the time the next question comes, it feels less like an interrogation and more like a therapy session.

"Walk me through what you remember," the interrogator says. "From your side. No judgment here."

The suspect takes a ragged breath, his words coming in fits and starts. "I—I don't know. I just lost it, I guess. It was late, and he wouldn't leave me alone. I didn't mean to—" The sentence cuts off, replaced by a nervous rub of the temples.

"Of course you didn't," the interrogator soothes. "Nobody ever means for these things to go down like they do. Sometimes, it's just... fight or flight, right?" He shrugs, conspiratorial. "They don't teach you that in school, but everyone's got a breaking point."

There is a psychological principle at work: minimization reduces the perceived severity of the crime, lowering both shame and resistance. By granting the suspect a moral loophole, the interrogator builds a scaffold on which a confession can stand—sturdy enough to support an admission, fragile enough that the suspect doesn't realize he's already halfway there.

The suspect straightens, some color returning to his face. The gap between them narrows, metaphorically and literally. The interrogator mirrors his posture, closes the folder, and sets the pen aside as if to say, We're off the record now.

"Here's the deal," he says, voice even softer. "We know most of what happened. We just need you to fill in the blanks. Nobody's looking to ruin your life over one bad night. The system isn't built for that. But the truth—it goes a long way. Especially with the DA."

For the first time, the suspect does not avert his eyes. "So—if I tell you, it's not as bad?"

"Exactly," the interrogator says. "You'd be amazed what honesty can do, even now. Trust me on this."

Trust me. The phrase lands with the weight of a lifeline. The suspect nods, minutely, as if coming to terms with something inevitable.

There is nothing accidental in this progression. In the literature of criminal justice, minimization is well-documented as a primary lever for eliciting confession, especially from the naive or the vulnerable. By offering a moral exit ramp, it tricks the brain into trading long-term consequences for short-term relief.

Nowhere is this clearer than in the case of the Central Park Jogger. In 1989, five teenagers were arrested for a crime they did not commit. Isolated, interrogated for hours without counsel, each was subjected to the same minimization tactics. "It's not your fault. Just say you were there. You'll get to go home." The boys, exhausted and desperate, eventually complied—confessing to acts they never performed, implicating themselves and one another. The confessions held up in court, despite obvious contradictions. Only years later, after DNA evidence exonerated all five, did the machinery of confession become the subject of national scrutiny.

Back in the room, the same machinery whirs. The interrogator shifts tone, lowers his gaze, and lets the silence work. The suspect, emboldened by the offered empathy, begins to fill the air: "I didn't mean to hurt anyone. He just—he wouldn't stop. I tried to leave, but he followed, and I just—" Another pause, longer this time, and the words hang between them, unchallenged. "I'm not a bad person."

"Nobody's saying you are," the interrogator assures him. "Like I said, anyone in your spot might've done the same. You just got caught in the middle of a bad scene."

There is no need to press further. The suspect is now an active participant, seeking not just to explain but to be understood, to be forgiven. The body language is no longer defensive—arms uncrossed, hands flat on the table, breath less ragged. The relief is palpable, as if the act of being believed, even by a stranger, has shorn away a layer of dread.

The interrogator stands and circles behind the suspect, laying a gentle hand on his shoulder—equal parts comfort and custody. "Let's just get this down," he says, "so we can all move forward."

The act of confession is, by now, a foregone conclusion.

Minimization works not by crushing resistance, but by offering the subject a way to survive what comes next. It is both anesthetic and lure, dulling the edge of consequence just long enough to draw the truth—or something like it—to the surface.

In the annals of interrogation, it is one of the oldest tricks. And still, as effective as ever.

Some rooms are designed for comfort. This one is not. The air hangs heavy, stale and faintly metallic, unmoved by the whir of an aging vent in the ceiling. The table is an immovable slab, surface pitted from years of rage and regret, sharp edges still capable of drawing blood. The clock—this time an analog—ticks loud enough to gnaw at the nerves.

The suspect sits with hands flat on the table, knuckles leached white. His shirt, once crisply ironed, clings to his back and underarms with dark, spreading stains. His gaze is fixed not on the interrogator, but on the line where table meets wall, as if willing a gap to widen and swallow him whole.

The interrogator is in motion. Not the lean-in, casual orbit of minimization, but a staccato, looping circuit that carves the room into ever-tighter radii. He carries a thick folder—unstamped, untitled, but bulging at the seams. Every time he passes the suspect's field of view, he taps the folder against his thigh, a metronome of escalating threat.

The performance begins. He slams the folder on the table, papers splaying like a deck of cards thrown by a bitter magician. "We have witnesses," he says, voice sharp enough to score the paint. "We have DNA. We have everything we need to put you away for twenty years." No room for doubt, no trace of empathy. Where minimization sought to shrink the crime, maximization throws it into relief—amplifies every allegation, paints the suspect's future in the harshest possible palette.

The suspect flinches, as if struck. A bead of sweat rolls from his temple to his jaw, falls onto the collar of his shirt, vanishes.

"You think you're smart?" the interrogator barks, rounding on the suspect with predatory abruptness. "Let me tell you what smart looks like." He snatches a photo from the folder—eight by ten, printed on matte, the colors oversaturated for effect—and slaps it onto the table. The image is a close-up: a face, battered, eyes closed, lips blue. "That's your handiwork. That's what we call evidence."

A visible tremor passes through the suspect. He recoils, then sags into the chair, spine collapsing in on itself. His breathing quickens—short, shallow intakes punctuated by ragged exhalations.

"You want to play games? Fine." The interrogator circles to the door and stops, blocking the only exit. He plants his feet and folds his arms, the classic silhouette of finality. "But you need to understand what you're up against. This isn't TV. There's no magical lawyer about to walk in and save you." He takes three slow steps forward, closing the distance until his knees nearly graze the edge of the table.

The suspect looks up, voice tiny. "I—I didn't do anything. I don't even know her."

"Bullshit." The interrogator slams the table so hard that the analog clock rattles on its nail. "Your prints are all over the scene. We have you on camera. And just so you know? She's talking. She's got your story, in detail."

The suspect's hands twitch, as if to shield himself, but he aborts the motion and returns them to the table, fingers interlaced so tight they're almost fused.

In maximization, the tactics are blunt-force: the physical domination of space, the volume of voice, the threat of consequences magnified beyond all proportion. The goal is not to make confession easy, but to render it inevitable. By painting the worst-case scenario in vivid color, the interrogator strips the suspect of hope, of alternatives. There is only confession, or oblivion.

The interrogator draws closer, his voice dropping to a lethal whisper. "You see this folder? This is your life, right here. Every bad decision, every screw-up, every moment you thought no one was watching? We have it all. And when the DA reads this, there's only one way out that doesn't end with you eating jello through a straw for the next two decades."

He fans out the papers: printouts, crime scene diagrams, mock-ups—some real, some generated for the show. The suspect's eyes dart between them, desperate to find an error, a loophole, but the narrative is watertight.

"You want to take a shot at explaining this?" the interrogator says, spreading his hands. "Because if you don't, they will. And you know what their version looks like? Monster. Predator. Animal."

The words have weight, battering the suspect's dwindling resolve. He sags deeper, gaze flickering from the table to the photos, then up to the ceiling, as if seeking mercy from above.

Maximization works by compressing the present into a tunnel: no future but the one offered, no past but the one dictated by the evidence at hand. It weaponizes fear, paints the justice system as an impersonal juggernaut, unstoppable, indifferent to tears or pleas. For the innocent, it is a waking nightmare. For the guilty, it is a preview of the abyss.

One of the most infamous cases: Jeffrey Wigand, the tobacco whistleblower. In his first major interrogation, the pressure was so relentless—threats of legal destruction, images of ruined careers, lives laid waste—that he broke, confessing to crimes he'd never committed. Only later, when the deception was exposed, did the narrative unravel. The confession was a product of desperation, not guilt.

Back in the room, the suspect's voice is nearly gone. "Please. I'll—just tell me what you want. I'll do whatever."

"That's more like it," the interrogator says, tone instantly softening to a mockery of reasonableness. He sits down, making a show of pushing the photos aside. "We're not monsters here. We're just doing our job. Help us out, and you help yourself. Make sense?"

The suspect nods, a small, involuntary gesture. The fight is over; only the surrender remains.

The interrogator leans in, elbows on the table, voice gentle now. "Tell us how it happened. Not the fantasy version. The truth. You'll feel better, I promise."

It is a lie, but it is the only comfort offered. The suspect hesitates, then begins to talk. The narrative that emerges may not match the facts, but it will be enough for a signed confession.

In maximization, the confession is an escape hatch: the only way to end the onslaught. Once given, it cannot be taken back, not even when the air is clear and the voices are gone.

The clock ticks on, a metronome for the breaking of wills.

Interrogation rarely ends in spectacle. More often, it is a slow, methodical attrition—a process less like battle and more like water wearing away stone. The room is unchanged from before: blank walls, unyielding chairs, air tinged with a tang of recycled sweat and disinfectant. But now, the threat is not physical or emotional; it is logical, relentless, a chess game played in a language of traps and feints.

The suspect has been in the room for hours. He slumps low in the chair, eyes half-lidded, wrists resting slack atop the battered table. Every so often, he shakes himself awake with a tiny, embarrassed jerk, as if caught dozing in a high school classroom. The interrogator faces him from the other side, legal pad open and uncapped pen poised but motionless.

"Let's go over this again," the interrogator says, voice devoid of inflection. "You said you didn't know the victim, but your phone records put you in the same location three times that week. Explain that for me."

The suspect blinks, rubs at his eyes. "I don't know. Maybe—maybe we had a class together or something."

"Okay." The interrogator nods, makes a show of thinking, but does not write. "So you're saying the meetings were random? Coincidence?"

The suspect nods, a little too eagerly.

The interrogator lifts the pen and taps it against his pad. "That's one possibility," he agrees. "The other is you were following her." No accusation, just an alternate version, delivered in the same neutral tone. "Which is it?"

The suspect, caught between two unflattering explanations, hesitates. "I guess—I don't know. Maybe I noticed her once, but I wasn't following her."

"Let's clarify," the interrogator says, as if genuinely seeking to help. "Did you plan this beforehand, or did you just see her and react?"

The suspect opens his mouth, then closes it. The line of questioning has closed off all other exits. Either he is a schemer, or he is a person of weak impulse. No third option is on the table.

"It wasn't like that," he protests, feebly.

The interrogator waits. Silence, weaponized. After a full minute, he repeats the question: "Was it premeditated, or was it a heat-of-the-moment thing?"

"I—I guess it was the moment," the suspect finally mumbles.

Now the pen moves, slow and deliberate. The interrogator writes only when the answers incriminate. Every denial is met with a tap, a nod, a return to the original question, reframed and presented anew: If not A, then B. If not B, then A. It is a logic gate, a feedback loop designed to close tighter with each circuit.

This is the narrative trap, and it is as old as the art of interrogation. By offering only two explanations—both damning—the interrogator forces the suspect into a cognitive tunnel. The instinct is to pick the lesser of two evils, the least incriminating option. Over hours, fatigue lowers defenses, and the brain seeks the path of least resistance. Denial becomes too difficult; the "less bad" answer is accepted, and from there, the next confession is easier.

The interrogator flips to a fresh page, makes a show of resetting. "Let's talk about the night in question. You left your apartment at 7:15, right?"

"I think so. Yeah."

"So either you went straight to the victim's building, or you stopped somewhere else first. Which was it?"

The suspect is cornered again, forced to choose a path he may not have traveled. "I—maybe I walked around first, I don't remember."

"So it wasn't planned?"

"No."

"Then why bring gloves?" The interrogator doesn't wait for an answer. "Was it because you were worried about fingerprints, or because you didn't want to hurt your hands?"

The suspect recoils. "I—what? I didn't have gloves."

The interrogator raises an eyebrow, but does not challenge the denial directly. Instead: "A neighbor says she saw you wearing black gloves. Could she be mistaken?"

The suspect swallows, voice trembling. "I don't own black gloves."

"But if you did, it'd be to protect yourself, right? Not because you were worried about getting caught?"

A pause. The suspect is unsure what to say—denial seems pointless, so he nods, a minuscule concession.

The pen records the moment.

This sequence repeats, endless, until the truth becomes irrelevant. What matters is the narrative, and the suspect's willingness to enter it.

The logic of the narrative trap is simple: fatigue breeds compliance, and every compliance is a step closer to confession. In the infamous Norfolk Four case, four men were interrogated, one after another, for a murder none committed. Presented with impossible choices—Was it you who stabbed her, or did you just hold her down?—each ultimately confessed, hoping to avoid the worst by picking the "least" bad option. They were told that only by admitting to a lesser role could they avoid the death penalty. All four confessed, all were convicted, and all were later exonerated when the true killer was identified. The narrative trap works not by revealing the truth, but by manufacturing a version of it that is easy to sign and hard to dispute.

In the present, the suspect's story mutates with each new question, as though the interrogator is editing a draft rather than interrogating a witness. The suspect begins to volunteer details he thinks will satisfy:

"Maybe I did see her leave, maybe I followed for a block, but I didn't do anything."

"Did you talk to her?"

"I don't remember."

"You don't remember, or you don't want to say?"

Another trap, another small surrender. "I don't want to say," the suspect whispers.

Pen to pad, checkmark.

It is almost anticlimax when the confession finally comes. "Maybe I did it," the suspect says, voice hollow. "I mean, I was there, wasn't I?"

"That's all we needed," the interrogator says, finally allowing a note of relief. He stands, gathers the pad and pen, and leaves the suspect alone in the now silent room.

No victory dance, no gloating. The game was won hours ago, when the suspect agreed to play by the rules of the narrative trap.

In the aftermath, the words linger, evidence of how easily memory and identity are rewritten under duress. The room resets, ready for the next story.

Sleep deprivation is not a side effect of interrogation. It is the main event. The suspect—mid-twenties, college dropout, dark circles pooling under both eyes—has not slept in thirty hours. His shirt is half-untucked, collar wilted, hair pressed flat on one side from repeated attempts to nap on the hard table. Each time his eyes close, the interrogator finds a reason to speak: a question, a cough, a tap of the pen. The conversation never stops long enough for thought to coalesce.

The interrogator has adopted the role of confidant, voice measured and almost clinical. No accusation, no anger—just a gentle logic, designed to unmoor. "You said you left the party at midnight. But your fingerprints—your fingerprints, right here—are at the scene at 1:27. That's not a theory, that's a fact."

The suspect's lips part, but no words come. He rubs his temples, jaw working. "I don't—I don't remember that. I went home."

The interrogator nods, as if confirming a point to himself. "It happens, you know. People blank on stressful nights. Sometimes the mind protects itself by blocking out the worst parts."

A pause. The interrogator lets the words breathe. The suspect swallows, then shakes his head. "No, I—I would remember. I didn't go back out."

"Memory's a funny thing," the interrogator replies, still gentle. "Sometimes, the body remembers even when the mind won't. You ever wake up and not recall how you got to bed?"

The suspect's gaze drops to the table. "Yeah, but that's—when I've been drinking. I wasn't even that drunk."

The interrogator lays out the evidence, stacking each piece with the deliberate patience of a chess master. "You were at the party. You left. Your car was seen driving back in the direction of the scene. Your prints are there. The timeline fits, but you say you don't remember. I believe you. But we have to face facts. Something happened in that missing hour."

The suspect trembles, just a little. He folds his arms across his chest and squeezes, as if hoping pressure alone could hold him together. "What if I just—I don't know, sleepwalked or something? It's crazy, right?"

"It's not crazy at all," the interrogator soothes. "Sometimes, people do things they can't accept. And so the mind erases it. Or buries it." He leans forward, elbows on table, hands steepled. "But you're not a monster. If you did this, there's a reason. Maybe you were scared, maybe you were angry, maybe you just snapped. But you don't have to live with the not knowing. We can help you get to the bottom of it."

The suspect closes his eyes, kneading his forehead with the heel of his hand. "I just want to sleep," he whispers.

"We'll get you a blanket and a cot, soon as you help us fill in the gaps. Otherwise, it's just more questions. More uncertainty. Nobody wants that."

This is the blackout confession: the engineered creation of memory distrust syndrome, in which the suspect comes to doubt not only their recollection, but the very mechanisms by which memory is made. The interrogator introduces a wedge, and every time the suspect tries to shore up his story, the wedge widens.

"How else would your fingerprints be there?" the interrogator repeats. "You tell me. Because if you can't, the jury's going to assume the worst."

The suspect's resistance is worn thin by lack of rest, hunger, and the constant erosion of certainty. Each time he tries to recall the night, the details grow fuzzier, less distinct, until the act of remembering is itself traumatic.

In the early 1970s, a Connecticut teenager named Peter Reilly was interrogated for hours after finding his mother dead in their home. Exhausted, grief-stricken, and alone, he insisted he had no memory of the killing. Investigators told him it was common, after trauma, to block out the event. They showed him diagrams, walked him through "possible scenarios," and suggested that a blackout might explain the evidence. Eventually, Reilly agreed that perhaps he had killed his mother, and simply didn't remember. His confession was detailed, remorseful, and entirely false. Years later, independent evidence proved his innocence, but the confession remained—a scar he could never quite explain away.

The present suspect is no different. He rocks slowly in his chair, muttering, "I don't know, I don't know," until the interrogator interrupts with a lifeline: "Maybe you just snapped. That doesn't make you a bad person. But hiding it—pretending it didn't happen—makes it worse."

The suspect looks up, eyes swimming. "If I say I did it, can I sleep?"

The interrogator nods. "Of course. Just help us understand. That's all we ask."

The confession that follows is dreamlike, full of qualifiers and gaps, as if spoken by someone else. The suspect admits to being there, maybe to pushing, maybe to yelling. Maybe he even threw the punch. He doesn't remember, but if the evidence says he did, then who is he to argue?

The statement is signed, witnessed, and the suspect is led out, unsteady on his feet, to a cell with a thin mattress and the promise of uninterrupted sleep.

Blackout confessions are not the product of evil, but of exhaustion. The mind gives in because it has nothing left to fight with. The evidence fills the void, and the story is written—sometimes in ink, sometimes in the empty hours between midnight and dawn.

The room, emptied of suspect, waits for the next mind to dismantle.

Sixteen hours in, the room smells of panic and old coffee. The suspect—mid-thirties, corporate accountant, married—no longer resembles the man who entered. Shirt stained with sweat and spilled water, pants rumpled, face gone ashen except for the burst capillaries around both eyes. He blinks at the interrogator across the table, but the gaze slides off, unfocused. The digital clock on the wall resets every few hours, a deliberate ploy, but the suspect doesn't notice anymore.

The interrogator alternates roles: now confidant, now adversary, sometimes silent for stretches that last longer than the suspect can count. The effect is disorienting, like staring into a strobe for hours and then trying to walk a straight line.

"How long have I been here?" the suspect asks, slurring the words just enough to betray the decay of his circadian rhythm.

"Not long," the interrogator lies. "We just need to wrap up a few things." A fresh pot of coffee is poured, ignored. The suspect is too nauseated to drink.

Every few minutes, the interrogator cycles through the techniques: minimization ("It happens, we've all made mistakes"), maximization ("This could ruin your life, your kids' lives, everything you care about"), narrative trap ("Was it financial stress or just a bad decision in the moment?"), blackout suggestion ("Maybe you did it and just don't remember. That's okay, it happens more than you think"). Each round chips away a little more of the suspect's grip.

Isolation is the master lever. No clock, no outside contact, no sleep except for the brief, fitful seconds when the suspect's head drops forward and the interrogator lets him rest—only to snap him awake with a "Hey, stay with me." After the first six hours, hunger and thirst become gnawing ghosts. After twelve, time dissolves. After sixteen, the need for relief—any relief—overrides every other consideration.

"Tell us what happened," the interrogator says. "Help us help you."

The suspect's head sags, voice hollow. "I don't know what you want. I'll say whatever, just—just let me stop."

And so, at the end of a process engineered for exhaustion, the suspect confesses. Not because it is true, but because it is the only remaining path to agency.

This is not an aberration. In laboratory studies, sleep deprivation of twenty-four hours can reduce cognitive performance to that of legal intoxication. Reasoning, memory, and impulse control all collapse in sequence. Under stress, the brain defaults to compliance—not out of weakness, but out of a desperate need to reduce the pain of uncertainty. The confession is not a moral failure, but a last-ditch adaptation.

The Amanda Knox case is textbook. In 2007, the young American student was interrogated for hours, denied a lawyer, sleep-deprived and isolated. At first, she denied involvement in her roommate's murder. But as the hours dragged on, the barrage of questions, contradictions, and suggestions wore her down. By 3 a.m., she confessed—inventing details to fit the theory pressed on her by investigators. Years later, all forensic evidence would clear her. But the confession stood for years, a monument to the power of systematic fatigue.

In the present, the suspect's signature wobbles across the page, barely legible. He is too tired to read the statement back, too tired to object even if he could. The interrogator thanks him, gathers the papers, and leaves the room without a backward glance.

The system is built on the presumption that confession equals truth. But under the right conditions—prolonged deprivation, social isolation, psychological assault—any mind will bend. The room is not designed to find what happened, but to extract a version of events that can be processed, filed, and forgotten.

The suspect, finally alone, places his head on the table and closes his eyes. The fluorescent lights keep burning. The room waits, a perfect engine for the manufacture of guilt.

Outside, the next file is opened, the next appointment set. The process will repeat until memory, confession, and reality are indistinguishable.

VULNERABLE PERSONS: TARGETS OF MANIPULATION

The room is a box, three meters by four, outfitted with neutral furniture and a faint odor of medical-grade cleaning fluid. It's walls are painted a color that designers claim promotes "calm receptivity," but under the fluorescent strip overhead, it flattens to the hue of old milk. At one end of the table, a teenager perches on the edge of a plastic chair, left leg jittering in nervous half-circles beneath the tabletop. His wrists are marked with a constellation of raw patches, each one a souvenir from days of absent-minded picking. This is Tyler: fifteen years, eleven months, and not built for this kind of endurance.

Across from him, the detectives present as a study in contrast. One leans back in the chair, hands loose and open, voice calibrated for empathy. The other maintains a professional slouch, ready to intervene if the first approach fails. Their files are organized, their pens at the ready, their names a blur in Tyler's ears—he's barely processed their introductions before the questions begin.

The first detective—call him the Good Cop, though the routine is more nuanced than that—smiles with practiced weariness. "How are you doing, Tyler? Need a water, or a bathroom break, before we start?"

Tyler shakes his head, eyes glued to a spot on the table where the laminate has peeled away, exposing a rough brown substrate. He mumbles, "I'm fine," but the word is shredded by the tremor in his voice.

The interview proceeds with surgical restraint. No one uses the word "interrogation," but both detectives are careful to log every deviation in Tyler's body language, every tremble, every darted glance at the clock high on the wall. The opening questions are designed to build rapport, but also to probe for weaknesses in the story Tyler rehearsed in the back of the squad car.

Detective One: "So, school's almost out for the year. You got big summer plans?"

Tyler: "Not really. Just...going to my cousin's, maybe." He wraps both hands around his knee to still its vibration.

Detective Two: "Your cousin's in the city, right? Lot of good skate spots out there."

Tyler nods, his anxiety momentarily displaced by a flicker of nostalgia—an old memory of an empty pool, the heat of concrete through ripped jeans. The Good Cop smiles, records the moment, then redirects.

Detective One: "We talked to your buddy Jayden. He said you two were at the arcade until ten."

Tyler's lips part, close again. He stares at the table.

Detective Two, voice neutral: "But the thing is, the store video says the break-in happened at nine forty-three. That's a problem, right?"

Tyler shakes his head again, but the gesture is smaller, less confident.

Here, the detectives begin the careful pivot to minimization. Their voices drop in volume, approaching the tone reserved for bedside admissions or awkward parent-teacher conferences.

Detective One: "Look, Tyler, we know you're not a bad kid. Hell, you've never even had a detention at school. But sometimes, good kids get mixed up with the wrong crowd. Sometimes things get out of control, and nobody means for it to happen. You understand what I'm saying?"

He does not, not really, but Tyler senses an answer is expected. He shrugs, a motion so slight it barely registers.

Detective Two: "We talked to Jayden, like I said. He told us some stuff, but honestly, it doesn't make sense unless you help us fill in the blanks. We get it—sometimes you're just in the wrong place at the wrong time. It happens."

The interview is now approaching the ninety-minute mark. Tyler's bouncing has subsided; instead, his hands are balled up in his sleeves, fingers moving in rhythmic, compulsive twitches. The detectives begin to alternate statements, narrowing the focus.

Detective One: "So, maybe you went into the store, but you didn't mean to take anything. Maybe it was Jayden's idea."

Tyler: "No, I didn't—"

Detective Two interrupts, gently: "Nobody's blaming you for going along. Jayden's older, right? Sometimes older kids push you into stuff."

Tyler swallows. "He just...he said it would be quick. I didn't think—"

Detective One seizes the momentum, "Exactly. You didn't think it would be a big deal. Maybe you didn't even know what Jayden planned to do. But once you were in, it was too late to back out. Is that about right?"

Tyler's eyes flick up, searching the detective's face for an answer. "I guess so."

The record will later show that, at this point, Tyler's only contact with the crime scene was via the video footage: a shadow at the corner of the lens, indistinct, possibly him, possibly someone else. But in the room, the narrative has shifted; Tyler is no longer denying, only minimizing his involvement. This is a direct product of the interrogation's architecture: relentless, but masked in concern.

Three hours in, the real pressure begins. Tyler's parents have not been called; no counsel has been provided. The detectives present a printout—an image freeze-framed from the surveillance tape, the shape in the background highlighted with a yellow circle.

Detective Two: "See, this could be anyone. But it looks a lot like you. You see what we see?"

Tyler looks, and cannot say for sure. "Maybe. I don't know."

Detective One, voice steady and soft: "You're not in trouble for telling the truth. In fact, it looks a lot better if you're honest with us now. If you try to cover up, it just gets worse. You know that, right?"

He nods. "I know."

There is a documented phenomenon in adolescent psychology called "suggestibility under authority," wherein a juvenile, faced with persistent questioning, will internalize the suggestions of adults—especially adults who frame themselves as helpers or allies. The prefrontal cortex, responsible for judgment and impulse control, is not fully developed until well into the twenties. For teens, the line between possibility and reality is thinner, more easily bent by pressure.

At three hours and forty-two minutes, Tyler's resistance has collapsed into compliance. His body is rigid, his eyes blank and unfocused. The detectives now speak less, leaving long stretches of silence. Into these, Tyler begins to pour his own narrative, drawing freely from the prompts he has been given.

"I guess I was there. I didn't take anything, but...maybe I didn't stop Jayden. He said it would be easy, and I just wanted to go home. I swear, I just wanted to go home."

Detective One nods, kindly. "That's what we thought. You're a good kid, Tyler. This is just a mistake. If you help us out, we'll make sure they know that."

He does not say who "they" are, but Tyler nods, grateful for the reprieve.

The confession, when it comes, is not a recitation of facts but a collage of what has been suggested: yes, he went in; yes, he stood watch by the door; no, he did not take the cigarettes, but maybe he knew Jayden would. He signs the form, his signature a shaky scrawl. He is told he can call his parents now.

There is a pause before the detectives leave. The room is silent except for the faint hum of the air vent. Tyler stares at the table, hands still trembling.

In research literature, the phenomenon is clear: Adolescents are two to three times more likely than adults to falsely confess to crimes they did not commit. The mechanism is both neurological (an immature prefrontal cortex, heightened limbic response to stress) and social (a deep-seated desire to please authority, escape discomfort, or simply end the ordeal). In controlled studies, teens confronted with even mild accusation will often admit to wrongdoing just to satisfy the adult in the room.

Later analysis will show Tyler's story is full of contradictions—impossible timelines, details he could not have known. The security video, when enhanced, places him outside the store for the entire duration of the crime. Jayden, when confronted with the inconsistency, immediately blames Tyler. Both boys are eventually released, but the confession lingers in the system, a data point that may resurface should Tyler ever find himself in trouble again.

The detectives exit, the room resets, and the next file is opened. But in the records of both law enforcement and psychology, Tyler's name will stand as evidence: of a system that prefers resolution to accuracy, of a mind not yet built for the adversarial logic of confession, and of the ease with which the truth can be manufactured from the right combination of pressure and suggestion.

For the rest of the evening, Tyler's words hang in the empty room, an echo of a story that was never his, but now belongs to him forever.

The walls here are tiled a faint green, the kind of color you only see in aging hospitals and halfway houses. The clock on the wall ticks so quietly it might as well be imaginary. In the center of the room, a man sits at the table, his face slack with a resignation bordering on patience. He is thirty-two years old, but his features are caught in a kind of perpetual adolescence: round cheeks, pinked at the tip of the nose; hair cut by someone who measures time in calendar months, not weeks. His name is Marcus, and he has been in this room for three hours, though he has lost all sense of what that means.

The interrogator is a functionary. Suit pressed, voice clear, hands that flick through folders like a dealer shuffling cards. He is efficient, but not unkind. The file in front of him is thick—printed statements, incident reports, a stapled appendix of "background"—but he has distilled it all into a single question: where did the missing property go, and what does Marcus know about it?

The interview starts with pleasantries, but quickly shifts into a cadence Marcus cannot follow.

"Do you know Ms. Reynolds, from downstairs?"

Marcus nods. "She has a cat," he says, pleased to have supplied a correct answer.

The interrogator nods back, scribbles something. "That's right. Ms. Reynolds is the one who reported the missing items. So, tell me again what you were doing last Tuesday evening."

Marcus's lips move as he processes, but the question slips off the surface of his mind. He tries, anyway. "I was—Tuesday? I was home. I had pizza." He remembers the pizza because it came with garlic knots, and he got to eat all six, even though he was supposed to save two for his brother.

"Did you go outside at all?" the interrogator presses.

Marcus hesitates. "Maybe. I think, yes? I took out the trash."

The interrogator marks the answer, then pounces: "A neighbor saw you coming back in at seven thirty. Is that when you took the trash out?"

"Yeah. Yes, I did." Marcus nods with relief. The conversation is easier when the answers are simple.

But the questions escalate. "Did you go near Ms. Reynolds's apartment?"

Marcus blinks. He tries to picture the layout in his mind, gets lost. "No, I just—our door is on the other side."

"So there's no way you passed her place?"

"I don't know."

"Because if you did, that's okay, Marcus. We just need to be clear. If you went down that hallway, maybe by accident, that's not a crime."

The words are soothing, but Marcus senses a test beneath them. He is not sure what answer is expected. "I guess maybe I did? Sometimes I get mixed up."

The interrogator smiles. "That's alright. See? We're getting somewhere."

Marcus's shoulders uncoil a bit. He leans forward, seeking the warmth of approval.

The pattern repeats, the questions coming a little faster now, laced with terminology Marcus doesn't always understand.

"What do you think 'breaking and entering' means, Marcus?"

"It's when someone breaks a window and gets in, like on TV."

"Good. Did you break any windows?"

"No," Marcus says, confident. "That's not allowed."

"But the door was open, wasn't it? Maybe you just looked inside?"

He hesitates. "I don't remember opening a door."

The interrogator lets the silence ride, counting down from ten in his mind. "Marcus, if you just tell us you went inside, nobody's going to be mad. But you need to be honest."

Marcus folds his hands together. He remembers a time, years ago, when someone caught him taking an extra cookie from the day program snack tray. He lied, got in trouble, and had to miss gym. He promised then that he would always tell the truth when asked directly.

So, he says: "Maybe I did. If you say I did, then yes."

The interrogator does not react, just makes a note.

Every fifteen minutes, the questions veer off and return, forming loops that Marcus cannot navigate. Some of the terms—"entryway," "testimony," "intent"—are explained to him, but the explanations are themselves abstract. When Marcus grows confused, the interrogator simplifies, or rephrases as a yes/no. Each time Marcus says yes, the interrogator smiles and writes. When Marcus says no, the interrogator frowns, or sighs, or says "are you sure?"—and Marcus, wanting to please, always corrects himself.

Over the course of the session, Marcus is shown printouts of items from Ms. Reynolds's apartment: a cheap wristwatch, a porcelain figurine, a box of novelty pens. The interrogator asks if Marcus has seen any of them before. He shakes his head, but when pressed—"Look carefully, are you sure?"—he sometimes says "maybe," just to be helpful.

At hour four, the interrogator begins to summarize:

"So, to make sure we're on the same page, you took out the trash at seven thirty, you maybe walked past Ms. Reynolds's door, and you maybe went inside, just for a second. Is that right?"

Marcus, exhausted but eager to finish, says, "Yes, that's right."

"And you maybe touched her stuff, but you don't remember taking anything?"

"Yes, sir."

"But if something was missing, you could have taken it by accident?"

He hesitates. "I don't know. Maybe."

The answers accumulate, like layers of sediment: each one flattening the contradictions, each one erasing the prior denials. The interrogator records only the affirmatives, skipping over the "I don't know" and the "maybe not" unless they serve to move things forward.

By hour six, Marcus is called a "good man" for his honesty. He is told that most people would have lied, but not him—he is different. Marcus straightens under the praise. When the interrogator tells him that all he needs to do is sign a paper, so that everyone can move on, Marcus agrees without reading it. He prints his name, each letter careful and deliberate.

The confession document is several pages, written in a register Marcus could never replicate. It is full of technical language: "unauthorized entry," "intent to deprive," "admission of guilt." Some sentences contradict things Marcus said earlier in the day, but these are not highlighted. When asked if he wants to change anything, Marcus shakes his head, trusting that what's been written is what he meant.

In the literature, this pattern has a name: acquiescence bias. Individuals with intellectual disabilities are four to five times more likely than their neurotypical peers to agree with statements put forth by authority figures, regardless of their own recollection or understanding. They are also significantly more vulnerable to suggestion, especially when tired, anxious, or eager to be liked.

In false confession cases documented over the past decade, adults with cognitive disabilities are represented at rates grossly disproportionate to their presence in the general population. Where most would ask for a lawyer, Marcus sees the interview as a test—one where the right answer is whatever pleases the examiner.

After the interview, the interrogator shakes Marcus's hand and tells him he did a good job. Marcus leaves the room with the faint sense of accomplishment, unaware that what he has signed will follow him for the rest of his life.

In the formal review, the case is closed in less than a week. Marcus's confession is cited as "clear and unambiguous," the product of a "cooperative and forthcoming" subject. No mention is made of his diagnosis, or of the fact that, when later asked by a social worker, Marcus cannot recall which day of the week the interview took place, or what the word "confession" means.

The room is cleaned and reset. On the wall, the clock resumes its soft, indifferent ticking. The system waits for the next subject, the next story, the next signature.

The air in the police station is thick with old sweat and old coffee. The interview room is windowless, more a converted supply closet than a chamber of justice. In the center: a woman in her thirties, Sarah, slouched so deeply into her chair she seems at risk of sliding to the floor. Her hair is unwashed, drawn into a loose knot that looks accidental. The dark crescents under her eyes could be birthmarks, but they are simply the product of too many sleepless nights. On the table in front of her, a paper cup of water shakes in her grip, making the meniscus tremble with each tiny spasm of her hand.

The subject of the interview is her daughter: age seven, murdered four days ago. Sarah is technically a person of interest—statistically, the family is always first—but the actual purpose is to see what, if anything, can be shaken loose from the rubble of her mind.

The first interrogator is female, late forties, with a voice engineered for maternal comfort. She sits with her palms up, elbows on the table. "Sarah, I know this is hard. I can't even imagine what you're going through. But we have to do this, for your little girl. Can you walk me through the last night, just one more time?"

Sarah's voice is barely above a whisper. "I've already told you. We watched a movie, she fell asleep on the couch, I carried her to bed. Then I did the dishes, and I went to bed, too."

The second interrogator, a man, hovers in the background. His job is to note inconsistencies, or to provide "contrast." He is silent at first, letting the first interrogator set the scene.

After the third repetition, he moves in. "So you're sure you went straight to bed? No calls, no emails, nothing?"

Sarah bites her lower lip, the skin there already raw. "No, just bed."

The female interrogator nods, reassuring. "That's okay. You're doing so well, Sarah. I know how exhausting this is. You haven't eaten, have you?"

Sarah shakes her head, mutely.

The session continues, questions looping in gentle circles, each orbit a little closer to the day in question. After two hours, Sarah's eyes glaze over. She loses track of time, loses track of her own words. When the interrogators repeat her statements back to her, she struggles to remember if she said them or just thought them.

At hour four, the dynamic shifts. The man takes the lead, his tone more clinical.

"Sarah, we've been going over the facts. The thing is, there's a gap. The neighbors said they saw your light on, really late. Like, past two a.m. Can you explain that?"

Sarah stares, uncomprehending. "I don't—I must have left it on by accident."

He leans in, but his voice is even. "People forget things when they're under stress. I know you don't want to relive that night, but it's important. Maybe you were just tired. Maybe you made a mistake and didn't realize it."

The implication is subtle, but it lands. Sarah's eyes well up, and she blinks rapidly, as if staving off a flood. "I just want to go home," she says, voice crumbling.

"We want that too," says the woman, quick to provide comfort. "But we have to get through this. For closure."

The questions turn pointed:

"Did you ever lose your temper with your daughter?"

"No—never. I loved her."

"Nobody's perfect, Sarah. Sometimes good people do bad things. It's not about blame. It's about understanding."

Sarah's mouth opens, then closes. Her chin quivers.

The interrogators begin to alternate tactics. The woman offers sympathy, telling stories of her own childhood mishaps, mistakes she made as a parent. The man injects doubt: "Are you sure you don't remember anything else? Maybe you just snapped, for a moment? Maybe it was an accident?"

Sarah folds into herself, arms wrapping her torso as if she could shrink enough to disappear. When they suggest that she might have lost time—"grief does that, you know, it can erase whole hours"—Sarah nods along, desperate for a narrative that lets her escape culpability, but also her pain.

At hour seven, she is weeping openly. She asks to call her sister, but is told "in a little while." She asks for a cigarette, but is told "not indoors." She asks for the bathroom, but is told "in a few minutes." The routine is one of deprivation—small needs denied, to amplify the larger one.

At hour ten, Sarah's mind begins to unravel. She repeats herself, often contradicting what she said earlier. "I just went to bed" becomes "I guess maybe I stayed up for a while." "I never hurt her" becomes "I yelled sometimes, but not that night." The interrogators mark each concession, building a case from the detritus of her fatigue.

By hour fourteen, Sarah is no longer sure what is real. The man tells her, "Sometimes people do things and can't admit it, even to themselves. The brain protects you. Maybe you blocked it out."

Sarah covers her face with her hands, sobbing. "I don't remember doing anything, but if you say I did—I must have."

"Do you want to tell us now, so we can help you?" the woman says, voice gentle.

Sarah nods, defeated. "I think—I think I must have done something. I don't remember. I don't."

The confession, when transcribed, is less a statement of guilt than a surrender to the logic of the room. Sarah agrees that "maybe" she went into her daughter's room, "maybe" she lost her temper, "maybe" she did something she can't remember. The interrogators thank her, assure her she has done the right thing. She is left alone in the room, hands folded and head bowed, until someone comes to escort her home.

Research into trauma and false confessions is unequivocal: the more emotionally invested a suspect is, the greater the risk of distorted memory, suggestibility, and eventual confession—even, or especially, when the facts point elsewhere. In one landmark study, over half of wrongfully convicted parents in child death cases confessed, despite no physical evidence linking them to the crime. Sleep deprivation, grief, and repeated suggestion are a toxic triad, warping the boundaries of self-perception.

There are protocols meant to protect the traumatized: time limits, mandatory breaks, access to counsel or advocates. But these are guidelines, not laws, and in the urgency to "solve" a case, they are often forgotten. Investigators convince themselves that the end—closure for the victim, closure for the public—justifies the means.

In the end, Sarah's confession is as much an artifact of her love as her pain. She could not save her daughter, so she tries to atone, even for sins she never committed. Her story joins the archive, another datum in the sprawling literature of interrogation.

The debate rages on: Is confession the gold standard of justice, or a relic of human frailty? The answer depends on the witness, the room, and how much of the truth anyone can stand to remember.

For Sarah, the night is over. The room is empty, the lights are off. But in the case file, her words will live on—one last gesture for a daughter she can't let go of, and a system all too ready to accept the sacrifice.

THE ROLE OF WITNESSES AND VICTIMS IN FALSE CONFESSIONS

The room is engineered for confession. Fluorescent tubes sear the walls and skin in equal measure, draining both of color. A metal table is anchored at center, the paint on its underside scabbed and peeling. Chairs are a shade darker than the cinderblock, designed for discomfort. At one end sits the boy: fourteen, maybe fifteen, his face scrubbed with the desperate cleanliness of someone told to look presentable. His jacket is zipped to the neck, the cuffs wet with sweat from where he's been worrying the fabric with his hands.

A detective sits across, perfectly aligned with the boy's gaze but just far enough that the table's width becomes a gulf. The detective's uniform is civilian, but the posture—back ramrod straight, fingers laced over a yellow legal pad—suggests nothing casual. There's a badge on the belt, partially obscured by a windbreaker, but visible enough to signal the hierarchy.

Between them: a silence that thickens with every exhale.

The detective breaks it first, voice sanded low. "You know why you're here, right?"

The boy shakes his head, but his eyes betray the lie, darting to the two-way mirror and then down at his lap. His knee jounces under the table, setting off a staccato vibration that rattles both the tabletop and his resolve.

"I'm going to say it again. We know about the graffiti at the middle school. We have you on video. I'm not interested in playing games. I'm interested in hearing your side before this gets worse."

The boy's hands clench into fists. His knuckles whiten, then relax, then whiten again. "I didn't do anything. I was just walking home."

The detective lets the statement hang, then nods, pretending to jot something down. He leans forward, elbows on the table. "Look, I get it. I was a kid once, too. Sometimes you mess up, you get talked into stuff. You want to be cool, or you want to show off for your friends. No one's here to ruin your life over a spray can, okay?"

The boy's head is still down. He's fixated on a nick in the tabletop, picking at it with his thumbnail until the skin at the edge of the nail turns raw.

"Here's what I see," the detective says, flipping open a folder. There are papers inside, but he doesn't reference them. "A smart kid. Good grades. No priors. You just got swept up. I'm going to level with you: the other two already talked."

The boy's head snaps up. "Who?"

The detective smiles, thin and knowing. "Doesn't matter. Point is, you're not the first in this chair today. If you want to walk out with just a warning, now's your chance."

There is a long silence. The detective watches the boy sweat, measures the pulse in the side of his neck.

"I—" The boy's voice cracks, then recedes to a whisper. "I wasn't there. Not when it happened."

The detective slides a piece of paper across the table. It's blank, but the gesture is heavy with implied evidence. "They said you planned it. You brought the paint. They said you wanted to get back at the principal. You even picked the wall."

The boy is blinking rapidly now, breaths coming shallow and quick. "No. That's not—someone must have told you wrong."

The detective sighs, a performance, then closes the folder. "Look, it's just some graffiti, kid. This doesn't have to be a big deal. If you tell me what happened, I can make sure it stays between us. If you don't, the school board gets involved. You know what that means? Expulsion. Cops at your parents' house. Your record's never the same."

The boy's knee accelerates, shaking the table so hard the detective's pen vibrates off the edge and lands on the floor with a faint ping. The boy jumps at the noise, as if startled out of a trance.

The detective retrieves the pen, then sits with forearms spread wide, palms open. "No one's trying to trap you. I just want the truth, so we can fix this and move on. Help me help you, okay?"

The boy wipes his hands on his jacket, leaving two dark streaks at the hips. He bites the inside of his cheek, then says, "If I tell you, does that mean—do I get arrested?"

"Depends on what you tell me," the detective says, not quite smiling. "But if you're honest? You probably go home with a warning. Maybe some community service."

The boy hesitates, gaze flickering between the detective, the mirror, the door. He glances at his hands as if expecting them to have changed.

"I guess I was there," he says, voice flat. "I didn't spray anything, though. That was—" He pauses, searching for the least damaging name. "That was Lucas. He did most of it."

The detective nods encouragingly. "But you brought the cans, right?"

The boy swallows hard, Adam's apple bobbing. "They were just in my backpack. From before. I didn't even think about it."

"But you handed them over when Lucas asked?"

A nod.

"So you helped. That's not nothing, but it's not the worst thing in the world. It just means you're honest, and you own up to your mistakes."

The boy deflates, shoulders collapsing inward. He picks at a loose thread on his sleeve, winding it tight around his finger until the tip turns purple.

The detective's voice softens. "Listen, I'll level with you. You're not in real trouble unless you start lying to me. I know you tagged the wall. I know what you wrote. I've got pictures. If you just tell me, right now, I can put in a good word. But if you keep dancing, my hands are tied."

There is a deep, shuddering breath. The boy's face crumples, his jaw flexing like he's about to cry, but he holds it in with pure force of will. "Okay. Okay. I did the first part. The outline. But I didn't do the rest. That was Lucas and Marcos. I just—I just did what they told me."

“See?” the detective says, like a teacher giving partial credit. “That wasn’t so hard. Next time, maybe just think about who you hang out with, yeah?”

The boy nods, his eyes unfocused, the edge of panic replaced with a blank exhaustion. The confession, when the detective writes it up, is a careful construction: “I helped my friends with the graffiti. I brought the spray paint and did the first part. I knew it was wrong.” The detective slides the page across the table and hands the boy a pen.

“Just sign here. Then you can call your parents.”

The boy hesitates, reading the words with a growing sense of unreality. His signature is a slow, tentative scrawl. As soon as he’s done, he looks up at the detective, as if to ask if that’s really it.

The detective smiles for real, this time. “That’s it. You did the right thing. I’ll let you know what happens next, okay?”

The boy nods, his shoulders slumped so low he seems to have lost half his height. He doesn’t look at the mirror. He doesn’t look at the detective. His gaze is fixed on the confession, the ink still wet and glistening. For a moment, the only sound is the click of the pen being recapped.

In the observation room, a supervisor marks the time in a log. In the hall, a secretary preps the paperwork. And in the interview suite, the boy sits, hands limp, staring at the signed document—the official version of what happened, now and forever.

When the detective stands to leave, the boy stays frozen in his chair, the silence rebuilt, thicker than before.

The room is smaller this time, and colder. A single bulb in a metal cage throws hard shadows onto the walls, carving every wrinkle in the janitor's face into sharp relief. The clock, set high and out of reach, ticks so loudly it seems to mark not just the hour but every passing doubt. There are no windows, only the same battered metal table, flanked by two chairs of different heights.

In the lower, plastic chair sits Eddie. The name is stitched in navy thread above the left breast of his work shirt, just beneath the faded logo of the school district. His pants are too short, showing three inches of sock above scuffed brown shoes. He holds his battered ballcap in both hands, rolling the brim back and forth in anxious rhythm.

Across from him, a detective sits with perfect posture, a pad and pen aligned at precise right angles to the edge of the table. No folder this time. The detective's manner is different, too—less edge, more patience, but also an unmistakable boredom.

"Do you know why you're here, Eddie?" the detective asks, voice soft and slow.

Eddie frowns at the table. "Because you said," he begins, then stops, uncertain. "Because you said I did something wrong?"

The detective's lips curl in what passes for a smile. "We're just talking. I know it's been a long day." He glances at the clock—thirty-seven minutes past the hour—and back at Eddie. "Did you see anybody near the front office last night after you finished your shift?"

Eddie squints, processing the question syllable by syllable. "After my shift? I—I don't remember. Maybe? I sweep up by the gym, then I clock out. Sometimes I have to walk around the front to get outside."

"Right," the detective says, nodding as if this is exactly what he expects. "But you went by the office, right?"

"I think so." Eddie looks relieved to have supplied the right answer.

The detective taps his pen. "That's good, Eddie. That's helpful." He scribbles a note. "Now, the reason we're talking is, someone took some money out of the front desk drawer. After hours. You know about that?"

Eddie shakes his head, eyes wide and guileless. "No, sir. I don't have a key."

"That's okay. Sometimes the door gets left open. Maybe you saw the drawer open when you walked by?"

A pause. Eddie's jaw works as he tries to remember, but nothing comes. "I don't think so," he says, uncertainty thickening the air.

The detective leans forward, elbows on the table, voice dropping to a whisper. "Eddie, I'm not saying you did anything bad. Maybe you were just trying to help your mom with her bills, yeah?"

At the mention of his mother, Eddie's face lights up—then clouds, as the implication dawns. "No! My mom's got medicine, but we go to the place on 14th. I don't take money."

The detective raises both hands, palms out. "Nobody's saying you stole anything. Sometimes people get desperate. Or maybe someone else asked you to do it. Did anyone ever ask you to get money for them?"

Eddie's face goes blank. "No, sir. I don't talk to people much."

The detective nods, as if Eddie's social isolation is another piece of evidence. "Okay. But if you needed money, you'd tell someone, right? Or maybe you'd just borrow it and put it back later."

"I don't—" Eddie stops, looking at his lap. "Sometimes if I lose stuff, I look for it. Like my lunch, sometimes it's gone and I get in trouble."

"Right," the detective says, voice as smooth as syrup. "It's easy to get confused. You might have opened the drawer just to look, and found the money. It wouldn't be a crime, Eddie, not unless you meant to keep it. Did you mean to keep it?"

Eddie stares at his hands, twisting the cap. "No."

The detective lets the silence stretch until Eddie looks up. "You're not mad at me?" Eddie asks, hope blooming in the question.

"I'm not mad," the detective says. "I just need you to be honest. You're doing great, Eddie. Most people would've lied by now. Not you."

Eddie smiles, small and embarrassed. "Thank you."

The detective makes a note. "So just to be clear, if you saw money in the drawer, you would've left it, right?"

"Right," Eddie agrees.

"But maybe you touched it by accident?"

Eddie hesitates. "Maybe."

"That's okay," the detective says. "Sometimes people make mistakes. What matters is that you tell the truth, so we can get you back to work. You want to go back to work, don't you?"

Eddie brightens. "Yes, sir. I like it there. They let me have my own key."

"Good. Then we just need to sign something that says what you told me, and then you're done."

Eddie nods, eager for the ordeal to end. His shoulders droop with relief, and the tension drains out of his hands.

The detective spends a few minutes writing, every so often glancing up at the clock, as if to keep pace with some external schedule. The final document is two pages, single spaced. The detective reads it aloud, but at a brisk clip; Eddie's eyes glaze over after the first few sentences. The words “confess,” “intent,” and “unauthorized entry” are pronounced with care, but Eddie doesn’t react.

At the end, the detective points to the bottom of the page. “Just sign here, Eddie. That’s all you have to do.”

Eddie takes the pen, hesitates, then prints his name in careful block letters, tongue pressed to the corner of his mouth. The detective blots the signature with a sheet of paper, then stands.

“Thank you, Eddie. You did the right thing. Someone will come in to take you home.”

Eddie’s face crumples into a relieved, gap-toothed smile. “Can I call my mom now?”

The detective nods, but before Eddie can process this, two officers enter. One of them gestures for Eddie to stand, and when he does, they handcuff him with a perfunctory efficiency. Eddie does not resist. “Am I going home now?” he asks, voice small.

One of the officers says, “Yes, we’re just going to stop by the station first.”

Eddie nods, reassured. "Okay. I'll tell my mom I did good?"

"That's right," the officer says. "You did real good."

Eddie walks out, ducking to clear the doorframe, his hands awkwardly pinned behind him. The cap is left on the table, spinning in slow, widening circles.

In the now-empty room, the clock ticks on, a metronome counting down to the next confession.

This room is identical to the others, yet nothing about it is neutral. The air is heavy with the vapor of spent tears and instant coffee. The walls, always an indifferent off-white, seem to close in with the slow, deliberate pressure of a vice. The woman at the table has given up on appearance: her hair is a tangle, her sweatshirt is inside-out, and her skin is splotched with the aftermath of crying jags too numerous to count.

On the table: a tissue box, emptied of half its contents. In her hands, a tissue twisted into a damp, translucent cord. She keeps winding it tighter, as if she can squeeze the feeling out through sheer force.

The detective is older, gray at the temples, his manner more like a school counselor than a cop. He offers her a fresh cup of coffee, and when she refuses, leaves it within easy reach, the steam drawing spirals that fade into the harsh overhead light. He waits until she's used three more tissues before starting.

"Thank you for talking with us again, Karen. I know this is hard."

She nods, eyes fixed on the rim of the paper cup in front of her. When she speaks, her voice is so dry it rasps. "I just want to help. I want to help you find out what happened."

He nods, eyes soft and sad. "We want that too. For him, and for you."

She blinks, and in that fraction of a second, the grief wells up and nearly overtakes her. She blots at her face with the tissue, but it does little to stop the flow. "I just—" she starts, then stops.

He waits, giving her time.

After a long minute, she steadies herself. "I just wish I could remember it different."

"That's understandable," he says. "Nobody expects you to be perfect. You lost someone you cared about very much."

Karen nods, but then shakes her head, as if both agreeing and disagreeing at once. "I didn't want him to die. I never wanted that."

"Of course you didn't." The detective's voice is warm, inviting. "You loved him. Sometimes love just gets messy. Sometimes people fight, or say things they wish they could take back." He glances at the notepad in front of him, more prop than tool. "Did you guys fight, that last night?"

She closes her eyes, the muscles at her jawline clenching so hard it looks painful. "We fought a lot," she admits. "But not like— not like that."

"What about?"

She exhales, a slow, rattling breath. "Money. The house. He said I spent too much, I said he drank too much. Same stuff as always."

He waits, letting the silence do half the work.

"We yelled," she continues. "He threw a glass at the wall, but not at me. I yelled back. Then he went out to the porch for a smoke." She's talking faster now, as if momentum will keep her from falling apart. "I went upstairs and slammed the door. I didn't come down until morning, and— and then he was gone."

The detective's gaze is steady, nonjudgmental. "That's helpful, Karen. Thank you." He leans in, dropping his voice to a near-whisper. "Can I ask—had he ever threatened to hurt himself before?"

Karen looks up, startled. "No. Never. He— he liked to make threats, but never like that." She catches herself, then corrects: "Not about himself. Just about how I would end up alone if I kept acting crazy."

"Did he ever hit you?"

She shakes her head so hard her hair flies. "No. I mean, he could yell, but he never— I was never scared of him."

"Were you scared for him?"

She hesitates. "Sometimes," she admits. "When he was drunk. He'd get, like, sad. Not mean, just... sad."

The detective nods, as if this confirms something already in evidence. "Did you ever feel like you couldn't take it anymore? That you wanted it all to stop?"

Karen's eyes widen, then well up again. "No. I mean, yes, but not— I never wanted him gone."

"That's understandable," the detective says, his tone unchanged. "People say things in the heat of the moment. Sometimes they even act without thinking. We're not here to judge. We just want to help you move on."

The word "help" repeats in the air, echoing back at Karen with the hollow resonance of an empty promise.

"Can you tell me what happened after you slammed the door?" he asks, shifting the notepad closer. "You said you didn't come out until morning, but the neighbors saw you on the porch at midnight."

Karen frowns, her memory a tangle. "I— maybe I went down for a minute? I don't really remember. I was so tired, I just wanted to sleep."

The detective writes this down. "It's okay. Sometimes, when people are upset, they lose track of time. Or even forget what they did. It's not your fault."

She nods, grateful for the absolution, even as her hands tremble anew.

"We're just trying to make sense of a very sad situation," he continues. "Now, this is a hard question, but I need you to answer honestly, okay? Did you push him on the porch?"

She looks up, shocked. “No! I mean— I don’t remember even seeing him.”

The detective’s voice stays gentle, but the pressure increases. “The thing is, Karen, we found skin cells under his fingernails. Sometimes, when people fight, even a little, there’s a struggle. It doesn’t mean you’re a bad person. Sometimes it’s self-defense, or an accident.”

She stares at him, paralyzed.

“Is there any way, any chance, you two struggled and you just don’t remember?”

She shakes her head, then stops, uncertain. “I don’t— I can’t—”

“It’s okay,” the detective says. “It’s common to block out traumatic things. If you did, we just want to help you get past it.”

The room closes in tighter. The overhead bulb hums, and the clock on the wall advances in slow-motion ticks. Karen pulls a new tissue from the box, but it disintegrates in her hands. “I just want to go home,” she says, not to the detective but to the ceiling, or maybe herself.

"You will," the detective says. "But you need to help us fill in the blanks."

She closes her eyes and tries to reconstruct the night, but her memories are muddled: the fight, the slam of the door, the dry mouth and pounding heart as she lay awake upstairs. She remembers going to the bathroom at one point. Maybe she looked out the window. Maybe she went to the porch. The gaps between moments are elastic, expanding and snapping back at random.

"I might have," she whispers, not sure if she's speaking aloud. "I don't remember."

The detective nods as if this is the answer he expected. "That's okay. Sometimes the mind protects us from things we can't handle. You're doing great, Karen. I just need you to say it clearly for the record. Did you have a struggle on the porch?"

She hesitates, then, in a voice barely audible, says: "Maybe I did."

"Did you push him?"

"I— I don't know. Maybe."

The detective writes, then sets the pen down. "That's all I needed. You're helping, Karen. Really."

She looks at him, eyes wide and red. "Am I going to jail?"

He shakes his head, soft but firm. "Not if you keep being honest. I'm proud of you for telling the truth. It takes courage."

She looks away, ashamed and relieved in equal measure. "I just want this to be over."

"It will be. Soon."

He stands, leaves her with the coffee and the tissues, and exits the room. Through the glass, an observer marks the time and adds a note to the file: "Subject compliant, responsive. Narrative consistent with evidence. Proceed with caution re: emotional state."

Karen sits alone, the echo of her confession hanging in the sterile air, another story fitted into the system's machinery.

At the end, she is left with only the wish she voiced at the start: that she could remember it different, or not at all.

The conference room is all glass and chrome, but it hums with the low-level stress of a courthouse anteroom. Every seat is filled: attorneys in sharp navy suits, uniformed officers with the postures of people who cannot sit comfortably in public, a handful of judges recognizable by their practiced detachment. At the front, a projection screen glows blue with a pie chart, its segments radiating outward in unequal slices—red, yellow, teal.

The forensic psychologist stands at the podium, one hand on a laser pointer, the other bracing the edge of the lectern. Her blazer is tailored, her hair pulled back to reveal a face that could either scold or soothe. The pointer winks across the screen, landing on the largest wedge.

"This," she says, voice amplified but controlled, "is the breakdown of false confession cases in this state over the last ten years. Note the plurality here—adolescents under eighteen. Next largest: individuals with diagnosed cognitive or intellectual disability. And here, a rising segment—subjects under acute emotional distress at time of interview."

There is a shuffle among the defense attorneys, an uptick in pens scratching on legal pads. The police contingent sits rigid, arms folded, eyes narrowed.

The psychologist clicks to the next slide: a bar graph. The blue bars for juveniles are three times taller than the gray for adults.

"Juveniles are three times more likely to falsely confess than the general adult population," she says. "This is not a question of character. It is a function of developmental neurobiology. The prefrontal cortex, which governs impulse control and risk evaluation, is simply not mature enough to withstand sustained custodial pressure."

A flicker of recognition passes through the audience. On the screen, a photo appears: the teenage boy from Scene 1, his hands fidgeting on the metal table, eyes locked on the detective. This time, the visual is freeze-framed at the moment of signature, the boy's face ashen and spent.

The psychologist narrates over the image. "In this case, the subject denied involvement for thirty-seven minutes, then shifted to partial admission after the introduction of minimization language. Not a threat, but a promise: 'If you're honest, you probably go home.' The subject's confession, now on record, is inconsistent with both the timeline and the available evidence."

Another slide: a headshot of Eddie in his janitor uniform. Below it, a caption: "CONFESSED TO THEFT—LATER EXONERATED BY SECURITY FOOTAGE."

She clicks the pointer. "For individuals with intellectual disabilities, the risk of false confession increases by up to four hundred percent. The data is even more lopsided when leading questions or promises of leniency are used. The subject may not understand the implications of confession, or may simply want to please the authority figure in the room. In this case, the suspect signed a statement he could not read, and was later released after video proved he never entered the office."

At this, one of the public defenders makes a tight, approving note. The police captain at the end of the table frowns, his knuckles whitening around a coffee cup.

The next graph is a scatterplot: dots clustering along a line, some circled in red.

"Acute emotional distress impairs rational decision-making by up to sixty percent, even in otherwise stable adults. We see this in trauma survivors, those recently bereaved, and—most importantly—those who have just lost a loved one to violence."

On the screen, a still from Scene 3: Karen, face wet and hands balled around a ruined tissue, shoulders hunched in collapse. The psychologist's narration is flat, clinical.

"After less than two hours, the subject moved from complete denial to qualified admission, and eventually to accepting a version of events suggested by the interrogator. Note the language: 'Maybe I did.' In laboratory conditions, subjects under acute distress will admit to acts they never performed, simply to end the session or please the interviewer."

She lets the silence hang, the facts suspended in air.

A judge leans forward, fingers steepled, eyes narrowed in concern. "Is there any evidence these trends are being addressed?"

The psychologist's answer is immediate. "Not consistently. Recording of interrogations is only mandatory in certain jurisdictions. Access to counsel is routinely delayed for minors and individuals with disability, sometimes for hours. Training in psychological vulnerabilities is sporadic, at best."

Another hand—a senior prosecutor, voice smooth and polite. "But you would agree that most confessions are valid? That the system still works, in the aggregate?"

The psychologist does not flinch. "Most confessions, yes. But the outliers represent hundreds—possibly thousands—of innocent people processed as guilty. The system is designed for closure, not always for accuracy."

There is a ripple of unease. The next slide is a map, red pins marking exonerations in the last five years. The room quiets.

"Remember," she says, gaze sweeping the crowd, "these aren't just statistics. They are people. Kids who wind up in adult prisons. Adults who don't understand the difference between a confession and a statement. Parents who confess to hurting their own children because, after enough hours, it is the only way to make the pain stop."

She flips the clicker, landing on a final slide: a black screen with white text.

THE MIND BENDS BEFORE IT BREAKS.

"This is not a theoretical harm," the psychologist concludes. "Every coerced confession—every confession extracted from the vulnerable—is a wound in the fabric of our justice system. If we care about accuracy, and not just conviction rates, we have to do better."

She steps back from the podium, letting the last words settle like dust. The audience is silent for a long moment—some stewing, some scribbling, some staring into the uncertain middle distance.

The session adjourns. The screen powers down. But the argument, now broadcast and archived, continues: in side rooms, in phone calls, in policy drafts. The system is slow to change, but change is coming—one confession, one case, one statistic at a time.

After hours, the law office glows with the muted warmth of yellow desk lamps and the blue-white haze from a pair of ancient monitors.

Paperwork is everywhere: on the desk, the credenza, even the floor near the door. An empty takeout box sits wedged between a casebook and a highlighter caked with dried ink. The whiteboard behind the desk is a tangle of arrows and bullet points—MANDATORY VIDEO, COGNITIVE SCREENER, LIMIT SESSIONS TO 4 HRS—each circled or starred, the product of long debate.

The defense attorney sits with his tie off, collar open, sleeves rolled. He holds a mug of coffee in both hands, as if it might bolt for the exit if left unattended. Across the battered conference table, the forensic psychologist from the earlier panel has traded her blazer for a fleece, hair now loose around her face. She pages through a thick printout, redlining sections and making margin notes in blocky, impatient script.

"You think they'll go for any of this?" the attorney asks, voice pitched low, as if not to disturb the towers of case files.

The psychologist doesn't look up. "Not all at once. But the four-hour max session? That's already in place in the UK and most of the EU. There's precedent."

He smirks, dry. "Precedent means nothing here until someone with a badge says it."

She points at a line in the packet. "Then start with mandatory recording. Half the states already do it. If the video's running, at least we can prove what was or wasn't said."

The attorney nods, and for a moment, his face softens. "You're right. The trick is getting buy-in from law enforcement. They'll claim it ties their hands."

The psychologist snorts, pages flipping. "What ties their hands is their own training. How many times have you watched the same script? Minimize, isolate, offer the out. Half of them don't even realize when they're manufacturing a confession."

He considers this. "Some do. Some just don't care."

Silence, broken only by the buzz of a halogen lamp and the scratch of her pen on the page.

The attorney stands, stretches, walks to the whiteboard. "You see this?" He jabs a finger at a circled note: ADVOCATE FOR VULNERABLE. "If there's a single reform I'd die on a hill for, it's this one. No kid, no cognitively impaired person, should ever be left in a room alone with a trained interrogator. Period."

The psychologist nods, the conviction mirrored in her own tired posture. "That's where most of them break. The social worker leaves the room, the parent can't be there, and suddenly the only voice they hear is the cop's."

He turns back, resting against the conference table. "You know what makes me sick? The cases that don't make the news. The janitor from the east side—Eddie? His story's all over the post-conviction appeal, but he's still in lockup pending review. They don't even want to admit the mistake."

The psychologist closes the packet, gaze sharp. "Of course not. The system doesn't want to admit how many convictions rest on coerced confessions. It's a house of cards."

He slumps into a chair. "Every false confession undermines the entire concept of justice. It's like a toxin. Spreads everywhere."

She regards him over the rim of her coffee cup. "Why do you do it, then? The pay's bad, the hours worse. And most of the time, the reform goes nowhere."

He shrugs. "Same reason you do, I guess. I had a kid on my caseload—sixteen, no priors, wound up in adult jail because he signed a confession after sixteen hours in the box. He didn't even understand what 'accessory' meant." He shakes his head, the memory a lingering ache.

The psychologist exhales. "I had a case in grad school—single mom, three jobs, loses her daughter in an accident. She confessed after the detective told her if she didn't, she'd never see her surviving kid again. Turned out the evidence was junk, but it took years to get her out." She looks down, blinking rapidly. "That one's stuck with me."

They sit in silence, letting the stories overlap and fuse.

Eventually, the attorney straightens, pulls a legal pad from the mess. "We should draft the procedural language tonight. Get ahead of the next roundtable."

She smiles, tired but genuine. "I'll annotate, but you have to make it readable for the suits."

He grins, flipping the pad open. "Deal. First clause: No custodial interrogation of a juvenile or vulnerable adult without an advocate present."

She taps her pen, approving. "Second: Sessions must be recorded, from first contact to final statement. No exceptions, no gaps."

"Third: Maximum duration, with breaks every hour and an absolute cap at four."

She adds, "Fourth: Mandatory cognitive screener at intake. Anyone who doesn't pass gets additional protections."

He scribbles furiously, punctuating each point. "We're going to piss off a lot of people."

She lifts her mug. "That's the job."

By the time the clock hits midnight, the proposal has a skeleton. Not enough to change the world, but enough to start a fight.

The attorney leans back, reviewing the notes. "We can't wait for the system to fix itself. Too many vulnerable people are paying the price for our inaction."

She nods, her expression fierce in the half-light. "Let's make them listen."

They raise their mugs in a silent toast, and the next round of reform is born—in ink, in coffee, and in the conviction that justice should bend for the people least able to defend themselves.

Outside, the courthouse is dark, but the office glows on, a beacon against the inertia of the system it hopes to change.

THE CONSEQUENCES OF FALSE CONFESSIONS

The police evidence room is cold and under-lit, the overhead bulbs rattling in wire cages and casting long shadows over the rows of battered lockers. The room is empty of people but alive with data, as if the history of every case file and every sealed bag of clothing has bled upward, pixel by pixel, to the single blank wall at the far end.

At dawn, the first figures snap into existence: a horizontal bar chart, its boldest band stretching farther than the rest, marked in a shade of warning red. The wall flickers and then holds steady, the numbers clean and insistent—27 percent, the legend reads, of DNA exonerations involved a false confession. The air feels even colder as the statistic lingers, the rectangle glowing against a background haze of case numbers scrolling beneath it.

Beneath the main chart, a secondary row of tables appears, rendered in grayscale with columns for Race, Age, Disability, and Offense Type. The "Race" column dominates: 62 percent of the names in the database are people of color. In "Age," a spike at 17, another at 22, a steep decline after 30. Someone, somewhere, has keyed in these numbers for an audience that will never see this room.

To the right, a pie chart radiates in segments of pale blue and dull orange. The blue portion, labeled "Juvenile and Intellectually Disabled," is a near majority, a wedge that crowds out the rest. Tiny footnotes at the margin clarify the point: Vulnerable populations are 4x more likely to confess to crimes they did not commit.

The only human presence is a cheap surveillance camera set in the corner, red LED winking, pointed toward the wall of evidence. Through its lens, every statistic is recorded for some future audit. But no one comes. There are no detectives on the benches, no city functionaries with foam cups and hangdog expressions. There is only the sense of inevitability—the knowledge that the numbers will remain long after the lockers are emptied, the evidence boxed and shredded, the cases closed or forgotten.

As the hour advances, the data refracts outward, mapping itself onto surfaces outside the precinct. In a living room in a nearby suburb, a slide show cycles across a flatscreen TV. Family photographs dissolve into one another: a boy in a soccer jersey, a mother at her nursing graduation, a Thanksgiving meal with too many side dishes. Superimposed on the montage, in a font more suited to government memos than memories, text scrolls:

"Average legal cost for post-conviction appeal: $60,000."

"Average income lost during incarceration: 35%."

"Risk of family housing loss increases 28%."

On the couch, a family (Marcus's) watches the parade of images in silence. The volume is off, but their tension is audible. In quick flashes, an uncle waves a report in the air and shouts something inaudible. A cousin stabs at her phone. Two teenage siblings lock eyes and then look away, as if the confession on the screen is contagious. In one freeze-frame, a grandmother holds a folded copy of the confession and weeps, her knuckles the same color as the bar on the evidence room wall.

Elsewhere, a home video plays: a child's birthday party in a park, a dog yipping at a cluster of balloons. Over the image, in stern white letters, the caption: "40% of exonerees were under 25 at time of conviction."

The camera cuts to the present-day party: the same park, the same child, now five years older and blowing out the candles with forced enthusiasm. The cake is smaller, the crowd thinner, and the boy's gaze is fixed not on the flames but on the family members clustered near the edge of the frame, some of whom will not speak to each other by the end of the afternoon. A brief, candid flash: an aunt and a grandfather, half out of the shot, arguing over whether Marcus is guilty or not. The sound is lost, but the body language is enough to animate the statistic from the chart.

At high noon, the county courthouse plaza is flooded with light. On the steps, the first protestors cluster in clumps: some with signs, some with leaflets, most with phones held up, documenting themselves and each other. The building's stone facade has been appropriated as a projection surface; a moving ticker loops in stark black and white, the numbers so large they are visible from the street.

"Public confidence in police: Down from 78% to 45% after high-profile false confession cases."

The courthouse doors open periodically to admit or eject officials in suit and tie, but their faces are obscured by the brilliance of the midday sun and by the ticker's slow, steady crawl. The protestors argue, chant, and live-stream, their words lost in the air but their message made literal in data: every chant is a decimal, every raised fist a percentage point.

Inside, the courthouse atrium is a hive of movement. Civil suits and criminal appeals share the calendar, the case numbers climbing higher each year. In a waiting area, three families pace past each other in uneasy truce. Overhead, on a digital display, case updates scroll by: "State v. Lee, retrial granted; People v. Gonzalez, appeal denied; Ex parte Jackson, new evidence admitted."

At a windowless corridor off the atrium, the scene changes: the state budget hearing room, the air thick with sweat and recycled paper. At a long table on a raised dais, a panel of budget officials listens to the day's first presentation. The witness at the podium is not a person, but a wall-sized screen that hums with the following sequence:

A bar graph: "Annual cost to incarcerate one person wrongfully: $2 million (includes court costs, retrials, settlements, medical)."

A histogram: "Average sentence served before exoneration: 15 years."

Next slide: a list of recent civil settlements, the zeroes running off the right side of the screen.

- "Davis v. State: $5 million."

- "Reynolds v. County: $3.2 million."

- "Jackson v. State: pending."

A voice from the dais: "These numbers are not sustainable. We could repair a hundred miles of road for the price of a single bad case." There are murmurs of agreement, the phrase passed down the table like a plate at a church potluck. The room is full, but the screen is the only presence that matters.

In the gallery, as the session proceeds, video cutaways play on smaller monitors: footage of crumbling school corridors, a teacher guiding students around buckets set to catch leaks from the ceiling; a mother guiding a stroller over a street so pocked and rutted she must lift the front wheels every five feet; a block of houses, half abandoned, the lawns gone to seed.

A second voice, sharper: "We can't afford these mistakes. We have to fix the system."

Back in the police evidence room, the wall of data persists, as if none of the day's debate, argument, or anguish can touch it. The bar chart holds, red and unyielding. The pie segments sit silent. The tables scroll slowly left, then reset, ready for the next printout.

There are no heroes or villains here—only the relentless march of numbers, the dull thump of statistics colliding with daily life. The room grows colder as the hours lengthen. The bar chart dims but never disappears, even as the rest of the room descends into darkness, the only light a faint blue from the surveillance camera, still watching, still recording, still waiting for someone to see what it has always seen.

The echo of the day's last sentence lingers: We can't afford these mistakes. Not anymore.

It happens before the first light, in the freeze-frame silence that hangs over the city's residential side streets. Maria Gonzalez jolts awake with her heart already racing, her breath snagged somewhere behind her tongue. For a split second she is seventeen again, still inside the boxy concrete holding cell, the air taste of bleach and fear. The shape of the twin bed, the texture of the worn quilt, the faded floral wallpaper—none of it registers at first. Her eyes track across the wall in wild, jerky arcs, searching for the camera lens, the slot in the door, the watchful shadow of the guard.

She clamps her teeth against the words that try to escape. The first sound is a gasp. The second is a hoarse, whispered "No, I'm free." It comes out like a question, uncertain of its own truth.

From the hallway, the sound of the apartment's radiator clanking to life, the pipes rattling just like the old jail's. Maria's pulse spikes again. Then: the distant bang of a car door, a man's raised voice, some neighbor's routine. Maria flinches, curling her knees to her chest, the defensive posture so well-rehearsed her body finds it even before her mind. She inches herself along the mattress until her back is pressed flat against the cold plaster wall—farther from the closet door, which remains, always, resolutely closed. She will not open it, not even to hang up a shirt. Not even when her sister, groggy and late for the breakfast shift at the hospital, asks her for a favor. The closet is a void she cannot explain, but cannot unlearn.

She lies there, every muscle tense, until the light from the street creeps in through the window and the city's noises drown out the remembered ones. She unfolds slowly, careful not to disturb the quilt, and sits on the edge of the bed, toes barely brushing the dust-swirled floor.

Downstairs, the news runs at a volume meant for a deaf grandparent, the voices clashing with the clatter of kitchen plates. Maria listens for her name, just in case—old habits. She recognizes the cadence of the anchor's voice even if she cannot parse the words through the noise. She waits for her niece and nephew to leave for school, the thunder of their sneakers on the linoleum a signal that it's safe to move.

She showers, gets dressed in clothes that still smell faintly of government laundry, and makes her way to the grocery store on the edge of the neighborhood. She cannot walk without checking every car that slows near the curb, every stranger who seems to linger on the sidewalk.

In the store, under the cold fluorescence and the endless chime of register beeps, Maria tries to remember her list. But her mind has other ideas. In aisle five, she freezes, one hand gripping the handle of her basket, the other reaching instinctively for the metal shelf to steady herself. The panic comes hard and fast, the old friend she never invited. Her palms go slick, her mouth goes dry, and she can feel her heart thumping in her throat.

Someone bumps her shoulder from behind—a hurried mother dragging two kids in mismatched shoes. "Excuse me," the woman mutters, barely glancing. Maria nods, cannot speak. She stares at the rows of canned soup, the patterns of red and white and yellow blurring together until she is dizzy with the effort of not running.

She waits until the aisle is empty, then leans her head against the shelf, breathing shallowly through her nose. "Not here," she whispers. "Not here, not here." When she finally moves, she takes a shortcut through the cleaning products and exits the store without buying a thing.

The world outside is too bright. She walks home with her face tilted to the pavement, every step measured, a running tally of the distance between her and the next possible safe place.

The therapist's office is on the fourth floor of a medical complex, the kind that smells of carpet cleaner and soft-serve coffee. Maria sits in the waiting room, eyes fixed on a children's magazine. Her fingers pick at the skin around her thumbnail, slowly and systematically, until it bleeds.

Inside, the office is a rectangle of muted earth tones, the furniture heavy and plush. Maria sits in the corner of the oversized chair, hands laced so tightly the knuckles shine. The therapist, a woman with precise makeup and a habit of speaking in double-spaced sentences, waits for her to start.

Maria looks at the carpet. "I can't trust them," she says. "Any of them."

The therapist leans in, arms folded on her notepad. "You mean people, or—?"

"Police. Lawyers. Anyone in a uniform. Even you, sometimes."

"That makes sense," the therapist says. "You had every reason to expect that help would come, and instead, it hurt you."

Maria nods, unable to meet her gaze.

The therapist uncaps a pen, twirls it absently. "I want to talk about trust, and about how betrayal by authority can compound post-traumatic stress. You're not alone in this." She gestures to a chart on her desk—another bar graph, this one from a journal article, showing rates of PTSD among exonerees versus those who were merely witnesses or jurors. "What you're describing isn't just fear, it's a wound made by the people you thought would protect you."

Maria considers this. She breathes out, slow and trembling. "It doesn't stop. Even when I know I'm not in trouble, I feel like they're waiting for me to mess up again. Like I'm being watched all the time."

"That's called hypervigilance," the therapist says, gentle but firm. "It's normal for someone who's experienced what you did. Especially if you were young, and it lasted a long time."

Maria closes her eyes. "I was seventeen," she says. "I kept thinking, my mom will come, my sister will come. But they didn't let me call. I thought if I just told them what they wanted, I could go home."

A silence, heavy as a blanket, wraps the room.

"It was never home again," Maria says, quieter now.

The therapist doesn't offer a solution, only sits in witness. "We'll keep working on it," she says, scribbling a note that Maria can't see and doesn't want to. "It's not just you, Maria. A lot of people carry this."

Maria nods, but her hands stay clenched, and her gaze stays fixed on the carpet, tracing and retracing the same worn line as if it might lead her back to a day before all of this.

When the session ends, she thanks the therapist in a voice that is barely a whisper, and steps out into the corridor, blinking at the white-bright light, not ready for the next thing but moving toward it anyway.

The state prison's visiting room is a slab of engineered sorrow: everything is concrete, sealed behind Plexiglas or bolted down. The cinderblock walls are painted a sullen, bureaucratic blue, so flat it seems to soak up the last of the light. Against one wall, a strip of orange plastic chairs is set behind a long, stainless steel counter, the surface scoured to a near-mirror shine by a thousand sleeved elbows and the institutional polish of custodial staff. The only splash of color is a vending machine in the far corner, its digital face promising neon chips and melted candy bars for the desperate.

On visiting days, the room fills early. The Jacksons know the routine, and arrive with time to spare. Mr. Jackson, still in his custodial khakis, carries the paperwork in a battered manila envelope. Mrs. Jackson, a church-going woman who once sold Avon to everyone in her block, now walks with a slow, shuffling limp, as if every step is measured to forestall the end of the visit. Their hands are dry, knuckles shining where the skin has split in the winter air. When the guard lets them in, they do not look up; they know the rules, and the chairs, and which one squeaks when you shift your weight.

The attorney arrives last. She is barely out of law school and seems to shrink inside her off-the-rack suit, but she has a voice that carries through every inch of the room. She pulls out a legal pad and sets it flat on the table. "We'll keep this brief," she says. "He's waiting." The Jacksons nod, say nothing. They watch as the attorney slides a yellow visitor's pass across the counter, watches the guard tap at his tablet, then walks them to the designated slot at the glass.

On the far side of the partition, Marcus is already there. His jumpsuit is blue, two shades darker than the walls, and his face is still round with a boyishness he cannot quite shed. His eyes, though, belong to someone much older. When he sees his parents, he lifts one hand in a slow, careful wave, the other hand already gripping the phone receiver.

Mrs. Jackson sits first, the plastic groaning under her. She presses the phone to her ear and tries to smile. "Hey, baby," she says, the words crisp and rehearsed.

Marcus smiles, lopsided. "Hey, Mom. Hey, Pops." Mr. Jackson nods, lips pressed tight.

The attorney positions herself between them, flipping her legal pad to a page with a red star in the margin. "Marcus," she says, "I have some updates." She scans the notes, voice low but urgent. "The Innocence Project has requested the full transcript, plus the original video. I need you to answer some new questions about the day of your interview."

Marcus nods, eyes down. He twists the cord of the phone between his fingers, just like he did with his shoelaces as a boy. "I remember," he says.

The attorney glances at the Jacksons, then to Marcus. "This is good," she says. "We're making progress."

Mr. Jackson interjects, "We sent the check. You got it?" He doesn't specify what check—there is only ever the one. Their retirement, their rainy-day fund, whatever could be scraped together each month after the mortgage and the copays.

The attorney nods. "We did. It helps."

Mrs. Jackson listens, hands trembling just enough to rattle the phone against the glass.

Marcus says, "You don't have to keep sending it. I'm okay in here." He lies, just a little, the same way he always did when he scraped a knee or failed a test.

Mrs. Jackson's voice breaks. "Don't say that. We're family. We don't quit on each other."

The attorney's pen clicks, quick and staccato. "We need to stay focused. If they get the DNA retested, and if the confession is found to be coerced, we have a shot."

Marcus nods. The attorney asks her questions. What do you remember about the detective's tone? Did you ask for a lawyer? Did anyone read you your rights? He answers, slow and deliberate, voice hollow but clear. His parents hang onto every syllable, as if the very act of recalling might somehow roll back the years, bring him back home in time for Sunday dinner and the roast his mother still makes every week.

After twenty minutes, the attorney packs up. "Next visit, I'll have more," she says. She stands, shakes Mr. Jackson's hand, and gives Mrs. Jackson a look of practiced comfort. "We're not giving up."

When the guard signals, the Jacksons hang up the phone. They press their hands to the glass, three palms in a row, separated by a pane so thick it could hold back the ocean. Marcus presses back, then lets go.

They leave without looking back, as always.

At dusk, the Jacksons' house sits at the end of a block of narrow lots and chain-link fences, the siding peeled in sheets by wind and time. The porch sags in the middle, the swing groaning on its last two links. Dandelions rule the front yard, their seeds spreading unchecked into every neighbor's grass.

Mrs. Jackson steps outside and pulls the mailbox open with a practiced, two-fingered pinch. Inside, there are four envelopes: one from the court, one from a credit card company, and two with no return address. The hate mail is easy to spot—it's always in block letters, the postage uncanceled, the message terse. Today's version: "MONSTER FAMILY" and "WHY DEFEND A KILLER."

She crumples the notes and pockets them before anyone inside can see. She looks up and down the street, but there is no one she recognizes; just two teenagers on bikes, one of whom points at the porch and says something she cannot hear, and a man in work boots hurrying past with a six-pack in a paper bag. The Jacksons used to have block parties, potlucks, trick-or-treaters. Now, the front steps are just for mail and the rare delivery from a grocery service.

She stands on the porch a moment, watching the street. She knows some neighbors believe her son is guilty. She knows others believe he is innocent, but think he was always "trouble." There are days when she wants to paint a sign—INNOCENT—across the front of the house, but instead she lets the silence do its work.

She unlocks the door, steps inside, and calls for her husband. No answer. She puts the mail on the counter, ignoring the envelopes that are not bills or ads. The house is clean, but it smells of old plastic and the last meal reheated from the freezer.

She finds Mr. Jackson in the garage, head down over the open hood of their car. The engine is half-disassembled, each part arranged on a towel by size and shape. He is not a mechanic, but he takes things apart anyway, just to remind himself how they fit together.

She rests her hand on his shoulder. "He looked good today," she says.

He nods, not looking up.

She wants to tell him about the hate mail, but she doesn't. Instead, she says, "Doctor's tomorrow. Early."

He nods again.

The next morning, Mrs. Jackson sits on the crinkling paper of the examination table. The doctor's office is not their regular one—it's a clinic near the bus depot, where the lines are longer but the copays are lower. The nurse checks her blood pressure, tuts, and writes the number on a clipboard.

"You been feeling dizzy?" the nurse asks.

Mrs. Jackson shakes her head. "Just tired."

The nurse says, "Well, you need to slow down. Stress will eat you alive."

Mrs. Jackson almost laughs, but her chest tightens instead. She coughs, once, twice. The nurse frowns, then presses a stethoscope to her back.

After the nurse leaves, Mrs. Jackson looks out the window. There is nothing to see but a parking lot and a stretch of highway, cars moving in both directions but going nowhere she would want to go. She closes her eyes. She thinks of Marcus, and of the years lost, and of the years still waiting to be lost.

That night, Mr. Jackson packs up the last of the cardboard boxes. They are not moving, not yet, but he's taken a job driving delivery for a local chain, and the van comes with the gig. He stacks the boxes—old clothes, tools, books he can't read anymore without falling asleep—by the front door. He does it after dark so the neighbors won't see, but he knows they already know. The porch light flickers, the bugs crowding around it in a storm of wings.

At 11:45, he pulls on a windbreaker, tightens the laces on his shoes, and steps out. He scans the street for trouble, as always, then climbs into the van. The engine coughs, then starts. In the rearview mirror, he sees the porch light sputter one more time before it goes out completely.

He drives to the warehouse, the night pressing in on all sides. He does not think about Marcus, or about Mrs. Jackson sleeping alone, or about the boxes waiting by the door. He thinks only of the road ahead, the next stop, the next mile. One thing at a time.

He repeats this until dawn.

Robert Davis wakes to a world that is always just a bit too sharp. The blinds in his one-bedroom apartment fail to hold back the glare, so he shields his eyes with the crook of an elbow, blearily watching the digital clock crawl toward ten. The room smells faintly of fabric softener and a less pleasant, metallic tang—a scent that never left after the day the water heater burst and ruined the old carpet.

On the bookshelf, in pride of place, sits a framed photo: Davis, age twenty, in a borrowed suit, grinning through a high school graduation. Next to it, a second frame, this one less celebratory—a plastic badge from the state penitentiary, his face rounder but already hardening into the lines of someone who's learned not to expect much from the next day.

He sits on the edge of his mattress, scrolling through his smartphone with one finger. The first email is a rejection from a rental agency. "After review of your application, we regret..." Davis doesn't read the rest. He knows it by heart. The next two emails are about jobs—one "We appreciate your interest," the other blank except for the word "Declined." The world is automated now, so every disappointment lands with mechanical regularity, leaving no room for false hope.

He closes the emails and opens the rental app again. This time, he goes through the motions slower, eyes checking the checkboxes he already knows by sequence. When he gets to the "Have you ever been convicted of a felony?" prompt, he taps "Yes," because there is no alternative. The app freezes for a second, then pings an alert: "Your application may be subject to further review." Davis smiles, bitter, and moves on to the next listing.

He stands, stretches, and pads into the kitchen. The linoleum is cold underfoot, and the fridge hums louder than a city bus. On the counter, a battered mug and a drip coffee maker are the only signs of life. The rest is as sparse as a motel suite: white walls, a single folding table, two mismatched chairs. The apartment is clean, but not cozy. He does not decorate. He does not accumulate. Everything he owns fits inside three trash bags and a pair of hand-me-down suitcases.

He drinks the coffee black, staring out the window at the strip of communal lawn. Three units down, a man in gym shorts is already on his third cigarette of the day, squinting at the sun as if it's a personal affront. Davis watches, almost jealous of the ritual. He considers going outside, but the yard is too exposed. He prefers the four walls, the illusion of a barrier between him and the rest of the world.

At 11:58, his phone buzzes—a calendar notification. He is supposed to be at his sister's by noon for the barbecue. The "family reintegration event," as his parole officer calls it. Davis puts on a clean shirt, glances at himself in the mirror, and wipes the sleep from under his eyes. He checks the lock on his front door twice before leaving, an old habit that refuses to die.

The walk is only four blocks, but each one feels longer than the last. The houses are newer here, identical in color and shape, the lawns mowed to regulation height. Davis walks fast, head down, passing kids on bikes and a pair of women jogging in matching neon outfits. At each intersection, he slows just enough to check for approaching cars, as if crossing the street were a test he might fail.

At the barbecue, the family gathers in clumps. Two cousins by the grill, his brother-in-law with a beer at the folding table, kids tearing around the yard in pursuit of a battered soccer ball. Davis hesitates at the fence, hands shoved deep in his pockets.

His sister sees him first. "Robbie!" she calls, waving with a spatula. The conversations near her taper off, then die. Even the kids pause, mid-chase, and look over.

He steps onto the grass, managing a polite smile. "Hey," he says, then adds, "Thanks for having me."

A niece—maybe twelve, maybe thirteen—looks up from her phone, eyes wide. She drops her burger onto her plate, ketchup splattering across the paper. Her friend whispers something, giggling behind her hand.

Davis tries not to notice. He walks over to his brother-in-law, who offers a can of soda and a handshake that lasts just a bit too long. They make small talk about the weather, the game, the traffic on the interstate.

From the far end of the yard, a voice: "I heard they let you out early, man. That true?" It's a cousin, half-smiling, but the question is edged with something between curiosity and suspicion.

Davis nods. "State said it was a mistake. Took 'em long enough."

A pause. "Bet that was something."

"Yeah," Davis says, "it was."

The conversation collapses, replaced by the sound of the grill popping and the kids' laughter. He sips his soda, watching the sky, counting the ways the world feels changed.

Overhead, a thin overlay appears, as if projected by an invisible hand: "EXONEREES: 30% LOWER INCOME, 20% HOMELESSNESS, 65% CHRONIC ILLNESS." The numbers float for a second, then fade, leaving only Davis and his can of soda.

He stands alone for a while, then moves to the table. He notices every eye that follows him, every whisper that halts when he draws near. He pretends not to care, but the tension in his shoulders says otherwise.

After half an hour, he slips back inside the house. He uses the bathroom, washes his hands for a full minute, then stands in the hallway and listens to the muffled voices from the yard. "He's not the same," someone says. "What did you expect?" says another.

He leaves without saying goodbye. He walks home with his face to the ground, every step a reminder that even outside, he is never really free.

Elsewhere, in another corner of the city, a former teacher sits in the lobby of a government building. Her hands are folded around a manila envelope, knuckles white with tension. Her name is called, and she rises, walking to the desk where a woman in a crisp blouse asks her to "confirm the details of your prior conviction." The teacher nods, answers the questions, then listens as the woman explains, gently, that the license can't be restored. "Maybe try a different field," the woman suggests, voice not unkind. The teacher nods, stands, and walks out, envelope clutched like a lifeline.

In another suburb, an ex-firefighter sorts through a bag of prescription bottles. The pills are rationed now, the co-payments higher than his unemployment check. He sits at the kitchen table, staring at the calendar: "Recheck appointment, three weeks." He draws a line through today's date, then closes his eyes, breathing slow, steady, the way they taught him in the academy.

In each of these places, the same overlay appears: "Average time to stable employment post-release: 5.2 years. 42% never return to work in original field."

Back in his apartment, Davis sits at the small table, staring at the rejected rental application. He holds the old prison ID in his hand thumb rubbing the worn plastic until the numbers start to blur.

He thinks about the barbecue, the way everyone watched, the way his niece dropped her burger. He thinks about how, when he laughed, it sounded like a stranger's voice.

He stands, sets the ID on the table, and pours himself another cup of coffee. He drinks it slowly, watching the numbers tick by on the digital clock. There is nowhere to go, no next thing, so he just sits, waiting for the sun to set and for the world to go a little bit softer around the edges.

The overlays fade. The apartment is silent, except for the hum of the fridge and the soft, persistent beat of a man learning to live in a world that isn't sure what to do with him.

The town hall is at capacity, air thick with sweat and the sour tang of old coffee. The folding chairs are filled—parents with crossed arms, retirees in camo baseball caps, high schoolers in t-shirts with activist slogans. In the aisle, a reporter holds up a mic flagged with the local affiliate's logo, mouthing silent notes to the camera crew behind her. At the front, a long table and three mics, each with a nameplate: SHERIFF, CHIEF DEPUTY, and DA.

The sheriff stands behind the podium, hands gripped at the sides so hard his knuckles have gone gray. He waits for the last shouts to die down, for the cell phones to stop recording. When he finally speaks, it's in a voice built for command but now stripped to the basics—yes, no, I will look into it.

A woman in the third row stands up, not waiting for the microphone to reach her. "How many more?" she yells, voice cracking. "How many more are you going to put away before you fix this?" There is a surge of applause, and a low, sustained boo from the left side of the room.

The sheriff nods, expression neutral. "We have already begun a full review of our procedures," he says. "I can't speak to ongoing investigations, but I can assure you, everyone is held to the same standards."

He glances at the DA, whose tie is two shades brighter than the rest of his suit, and whose left knee bounces under the table in a desperate Morse code. "That's not an answer," someone shouts from the back. "Do you even care?" Another voice: "Tell us about Marcus Jackson!" The room pulses with anger, everyone speaking at once until the moderator bangs a gavel and demands silence.

From the wall, a projector hums to life, and the data from the earlier evidence room reappears: "27% OF DNA EXONERATIONS INVOLVED A FALSE CONFESSION." The crowd reads it, out loud and in unison. A ripple of laughter, sharp and bitter, rolls through the room.

The sheriff clears his throat. "Mistakes were made," he says, and the phrase hovers in the air, heavy as a storm front.

After the meeting, the local news station picks up the action. The studio is frigid and blindingly lit, everything designed to wash out flaws and exaggerate contrasts. The anchor, a woman with precisely angled hair and the composure of a chess grandmaster, looks into the camera, then to the prosecutor sitting across the glass desk.

"Thank you for joining us," she says, tone set to cordial but dangerous. "Let's get right to it. The numbers are damning. What do you say to families who feel their loved ones were coerced?"

The prosecutor straightens his tie, offers a practiced half-smile. "We follow the law. We do everything by the book."

"But the book has changed," the anchor counters. "There's bodycam now. There's new DNA. There are advocates in the room. Why do the confessions keep coming?"

A pause. "I can't speak to every case. Some people—sometimes they confess because they're guilty."

"But sometimes they're not," the anchor says, "and we've seen, just tonight, at least three cases where the state had to admit error. So how do you restore faith?"

The prosecutor's eyes flicker, just for a second, off-camera and back. "We review. We implement new training. It's a work in progress."

The anchor's voice is soft but relentless. "Isn't it too late for the people already serving time?"

He hesitates. "We are working as fast as we can."

The segment cuts to commercial, the set freezing in a moment of polite standoff. The prosecutor exhales, shoulders slumping as soon as the lights drop. The anchor turns away, already scanning her tablet for the next segment.

In a quiet conference room just off the studio, two jurors from the Jackson case sit together. Their hands are folded in identical postures, the air between them heavy with shame. A producer, not much older than the jurors themselves, runs the audio for the confession: Marcus's voice, shaky but clear, repeating the same details over and over.

The first juror, a man in a Carhartt vest, shakes his head. "We believed it," he says, almost to himself. "I mean, why would someone say they did it if they didn't?"

The second juror, a woman in glasses with a smudge on one lens, sniffs. "They never showed us the video. Just read the transcript. It sounded real."

The producer says nothing, just lets the tape play. Marcus's voice grows more fragile each time, words slurring as the hours pass, each answer less certain than the one before.

"We had no idea," the woman says, and looks away, blinking hard.

The room is silent except for the low hiss of the audio, and the distant echo of the town hall, the TV, the world outside grappling with a problem that suddenly feels a lot closer to home.

The law school auditorium is full to the fire code, the walls alive with the sound of shoes on tile and restless programs flipping in anxious hands. At the front, a raised stage: wood panels, a line of folding chairs occupied by the faculty in their rainbow hoods, and a single, battered podium that looks as if it's survived a hundred years of oratory.

The midday sun falls through high windows in slices, striping the audience and making the graduates squint as they line up on the aisle, robes sharp and uncreased, faces alternating between wild hope and the blank terror of the untried. The dean gives the standard greeting, half-welcome and half-injunction, and gestures to the man at the podium: a retired judge, rumored to have once written his own closing arguments in verse.

The judge's voice carries even before the mic amplifies it. "Our system failed these people," he says, and it is clear from the hush that everyone knows what he means. "You know the cases. The numbers. The names that will not be erased." He looks out over the rows, fixing the front row with the full force of his gaze. "You are the first class required to take the new oath. A promise to protect—not just the law as written, but the lives behind it. Will you make that promise?"

The response, at first, is hesitant. Then a few voices rise—yes, yes—until the whole auditorium shakes with it.

He lifts a hand. "Please rise and repeat after me."

The audience stands, hundreds of black gowns rustling in synchrony.

"I swear to uphold the rights of every person, no matter their station, their story, or the mistakes made against them," the judge says.

The students repeat, stumbling at first, then stronger: "I swear to uphold the rights of every person, no matter their station, their story, or the mistakes made against them."

"I promise to safeguard the innocent as fiercely as I pursue the guilty."

"I promise to safeguard the innocent as fiercely as I pursue the guilty."

"I will never ignore a cry for justice, no matter how small, how inconvenient, or how late it arrives."

The words echo, then fade, replaced by the sudden, unexpected sound of applause—first from the back, then rolling forward until even the judge, so rarely moved, has to pause to let it crest and break.

As the students sit, the dean returns to the mic, voice slightly choked: "Let's get to work."

The Innocence Project office is a riot of whiteboards, half-empty coffee mugs, and the light hum of HVAC fighting a losing battle with the outside heat. At the center, a battered conference table covered in legal pads, highlighters, and laptops, cables winding through the mess like veins in a leaf.

Three lawyers, two researchers, and a paralegal sit hip to hip. The first lawyer, sleeves rolled to the elbow, scrolls rapidly through a PDF, reading aloud. "If we add a Miranda trigger for all minors and require an advocate in the room—"

The paralegal interrupts. "But only if it's enforceable. Otherwise, cops will just ignore it like they do in other states."

"Let's make it enforceable," says the second lawyer, already tapping at her keyboard. "Any interview without the safeguard is inadmissible, period."

The researcher, glasses fogged up from the heat, gestures with a pen. "We need a checklist, not just policy. A checklist that gets signed by every officer in the room, every time."

Laptops clatter, pens scratch, and three different colored Post-Its sprout up along the edge of a shared screen: "MANDATORY VIDEO"; "NO WAIVER FOR UNDER 18"; "CLOSE FAMILY CONTACT WITHIN 1 HR." They argue over language—"credible adult" versus "trusted adult," "shall" versus "must"—but the mood is urgent, not angry. They have lost too many cases to word games, and they will not let this one slip through.

In the corner, a battered Keurig chugs out a cup of coffee. The researcher stands, grabs it, and returns just in time to catch the last words of the proposal. "With these safeguards, we can reduce the risk by half in the first five years. That's our projection. That's what we tell them."

The paralegal highlights the line. "I'll draft the cover letter," she says.

The three lawyers look at each other, a moment of eye contact that is as much pact as approval. The first lawyer leans back, letting out a long, tired breath. "Next step: get someone to sponsor it."

"I know a state rep who just lost a son to a wrongful conviction," says the second lawyer. "He'll listen."

They smile, grim and determined.

On the wall, a whiteboard reads: "NOT ONE MORE."

The researcher picks up a marker and draws a check next to it.

As the afternoon light grows slanted and gold, the group sends off the first draft to the coalition partners, the whole room wired and exhausted, but already ready to move on to the next case.

Down the hall, the sound of a phone ringing. Someone picks it up: another new case, another family hoping for a miracle. The fight never stops, but for a moment, in the office thick with the smell of coffee and determination, it feels possible that the oath might hold.

Dusk falls over the plaza in a slow, blue hush, cooling the air and polishing every surface to a metallic sheen. Streetlights pop on in sequence, yellow domes blooming atop their slender poles, while the last of the day's commuters dissolve into shadow.

At the far edge of the plaza, a wall of granite rises up: ten feet high, forty feet long, polished so perfectly that the first time you see it, you think it's a pool of dark water held vertical. The surface reflects everything—the lamp glow, the faces of passersby, the autumn trees whose bare branches rake the sky. The only thing that does not reflect is the text: the engraved names, ordered by date and case number, each line a silent record of someone who died behind bars before the state admitted its mistake.

A group of exonerees stands together at the base of the wall, all ages, all shapes, all wearing the same slightly stunned look of people still not sure what to do with freedom. Some are with family, others alone. They stand with their hands in their pockets, or crossed in front, or awkwardly holding the programs from the dedication ceremony. No one speaks.

One man, older and moving with careful precision, steps forward and lays his hand flat on the stone, just below the name he has come to find. He traces each letter with a thumb, then stands back and lets someone else take his place.

A young woman in a borrowed suit laughs softly and wipes her eyes then leans forward to touch a name near the bottom of the list. She reads the inscription once, then again, lips moving soundlessly.

Another man, stoop-shouldered and pale, runs his palm over the length of the wall, as if to bless every name at once.

Above them, the streetlights cast their silhouettes in long, unbroken lines that stretch across the plaza and up the side of a nearby building, shadows that outnumber the living but never quite cover the words on the stone.

After a time, the group moves away, one by one, drifting toward the benches, the paths, the uncertain city beyond. The wall remains, catching the light, the sky, and the faces of those who come after, holding every story in its silent, unyielding memory.

REFORMING THE SYSTEM: A PATH TO JUSTICE

In the lexicon of criminal justice, nothing is more iconic—or more fraught—than the interrogation room. It is a stage for drama and a laboratory for human behavior, equal parts theater and experiment. The conventional version is as familiar as a prime-time police procedural: Four walls, painted an indifferent gray or the color of bureaucratic oatmeal, a single metal table, a pair of mismatched chairs. One-way mirror, check. Clock on the wall, always visible to the observer, never to the suspect. Overhead light fixed at maximum, casting unflattering shadows on every face and amplifying even the smallest twitch of anxiety.

This is the environment where most American confessions have been manufactured for the last half-century. Its logic is simple: Control the stimulus, control the subject. Sensory deprivation and psychological discomfort as tools of the trade.

In contrast, the "reformed" room—seen first in pilot programs, then codified into progressive law enforcement architecture—looks like the waiting area for a mid-range dental practice. The walls are a gentle, noncommittal blue. Chairs are ergonomic, the table is oak veneer with rounded corners. The lighting is diffuse, set to match average office standards for warmth. There are no mirrors, one-way or otherwise. Instead, cameras are mounted in plain sight, their presence signaled by a small, laminated placard at the door: THIS INTERVIEW IS BEING AUDIO- AND VIDEO-RECORDED FOR YOUR SAFETY AND OURS.

The difference is not merely cosmetic. In King County, Washington, after the new rooms went live, a university research group ran a randomized comparison: suspects were assigned to either the legacy suite or the "humane design" pilot. The results were immediate. Self-reported anxiety scores dropped by a third. The number of confessions judged by outside reviewers as "voluntary" jumped by forty percent. Most crucially: The rate of false confessions among vulnerable populations—juveniles, those with intellectual disability, those flagged for high trauma—was cut in half.

On a split screen, two scenes unfold. In the old room, a young woman with her hair pulled back sits at the table, shoulders hunched, hands folded so tightly the skin at the knuckles is bloodless. She stares at the metal surface, avoiding both the detective and her own reflection in the mirror. There are no props save for a paper cup of water and a stack of manila folders. The detective leans forward, elbows sharp, every question delivered in the cadence of a closing argument.

Across the hall, in the reformed room, a man in his fifties, balding and unsteady, is offered a cup of coffee and asked if the temperature is comfortable. The interviewer sits at a respectful distance, tablet in hand, and does not raise her voice. The subject appears nervous, yes, but he also meets the interviewer's eye and does not fidget with the furniture. There is a small sign on the wall reminding him of his right to have a lawyer present. The clock is visible. The tone is less adversarial, more akin to a therapist's intake than an interrogation.

The architects of the new rooms like to say the biggest difference is not in the paint or the chairs, but in what is left outside the door: intimidation, humiliation, and the implicit threat of violence. "It's not a trick," one of them says on a TEDx stage. "It's a reset."

The data, when overlaid, is stark. In the decade prior to environmental reform, County X averaged one new false confession case every 14 months—each with a price tag in the millions once civil litigation and retrials were factored in. After the reforms, the interval stretched to nearly three years. The line on the graph is not a gentle slope, but a cliff.

There is a school of thought that says such reforms "coddle the criminal." But the numbers suggest the opposite: As the rooms got softer, the confessions got harder—harder to dispute, harder to reverse on appeal, harder to blame on procedural error. Public trust, once hovering in the mid-40s on annual community surveys, nudged upward, year by year, until a majority of residents—across race, age, and party—said they believed their local police "acted in good faith during interviews."

But the most revolutionary reform was not spatial. It was temporal: mandatory recording of all interrogations, from the moment of first contact to the last signed statement. This did not start as a best practice; it started as a court order, after a wrongful conviction suit nearly bankrupted a small city in the Midwest. The idea migrated outward, jurisdiction by jurisdiction, until a critical mass of states (Illinois, then Wisconsin, then Oregon, then New York) made it statutory.

At first, officers resisted. Union reps warned that "big brother" would tie their hands, that suspects would "play to the camera." But in the states where video recording became law, something unexpected happened. The rate of contested confessions plummeted. Fewer retractions, fewer claims of coercion, fewer last-minute scrambles by prosecutors to salvage tainted cases. And, contrary to the doomsayers, conviction rates in serious felonies stayed the same—or rose. The difference was the confessions held up in court.

In one Illinois pilot, over 90% of recorded interrogations led to guilty pleas or convictions without pretrial drama. The video was the new gold standard. More than one judge, when asked about the impact, said: "It's like instant replay in football. The game is cleaner, the calls are fairer, and nobody gets away with blaming the ref."

But perhaps the strongest evidence for recording is in the rare but catastrophic outlier: the suspect who, absent a video, would have confessed to anything to make the pain stop. In the annals of exoneration, the "false confession" category is now almost exclusively populated by cases pre-dating the recording era. After, the graph is nearly flat.

Consider the following excerpt, from a real (now-public) interrogation, conducted under the new regime:

Detective: "We're not here to trick you. This is being recorded, you understand?"

Suspect: "Yes. Am I in trouble?"

Detective: "That depends on what you tell us. But you're not leaving here unless we're all clear, okay?"

(Long pause. The suspect looks into the camera. She bites her lip.)

Detective: "Take your time. When you're ready, just tell us what happened."

Suspect: "I wasn't there. You can check my phone. I left at seven, just like I said."

Detective: "Alright. We'll check. But if there's anything you're not telling us, now is your chance."

Suspect: "I'm telling you the truth."

Six months later, phone records confirm the suspect's account. The case is dropped before it even reaches indictment. The video shows no minimization, no threats, no hint of pressure beyond the standard-issue awkwardness of the room.

Now consider, by contrast, the transcript from a pre-recording era case:

Detective: "Listen, if you just tell us what we want to hear, we'll help you out."

Suspect: "Okay."

Detective: "Did you see the victim that night?"

Suspect: "If you say I did, then yes."

Detective: "Good. Now, how did it happen?"

Suspect: (inaudible, mumbling)

Detective: "Don't worry about the details. Just say you were there."

The rest is a paperwork formality. The confession, though later recanted, is enough to secure a plea deal. The case is never reviewed, the mistake never corrected.

The old room, the new room. The line is not just spatial, but historical—a bright demarcation between what the justice system once demanded of its subjects, and what it now demands of itself.

What does it cost to record every interview, to upholster a chair, to repaint a wall? Less, it turns out, than the price of a single wrongful conviction, measured in years, in dollars, in ruined lives. The lesson is clear, if not always popular: If you want the truth, start by making a space where it can survive.

The next frontier is not the room, but the mind inside it.

If the interrogation room is the stage, law enforcement is the cast. For decades, the script was handed down by tradition: seasoned detectives coaching rookies on the "art" of getting a confession, the sly pivot from rapport to confrontation, the calculated deployment of guilt and relief. Formal training existed, but it was haphazard—a patchwork of war stories, borrowed manuals, and YouTube bootlegs.

In the wake of a generation's worth of exoneration scandals, that script is being rewritten. Now, the point of entry is not the badge, but the classroom.

Inside the training annex of a mid-sized city's police headquarters, rows of officers—some in uniform, some in plainclothes, some in the faded hoodies of lifelong shift work—are seated at long tables facing a digital whiteboard. The instructor, a former detective with a PhD in psychology, stands at the front, laser pointer in one hand and a clicker in the other. Her voice is brisk, pitched for the caffeine-and-cynicism crowd.

"Who here has ever heard of cognitive bias?" she asks.

A few tentative hands go up. A detective in the second row raises his, then withdraws it halfway, uncertain if this is a trick question.

"Good," she says. "Now: What kinds of bias are we talking about? Anyone?"

There is a short, embarrassed silence, broken only by the tap of pens and the distant drone of HVAC. Eventually, a veteran sergeant volunteers, "Like, maybe, if you already think the suspect is guilty, you hear what you want to hear?"

The instructor lights up. "Exactly. Confirmation bias. But there are others. Expectancy bias, memory contamination, tunnel vision." She cycles through slides: mug shots morphing with each retelling, transcripts edited by memory until the original is unrecognizable. "Our job is to stop thinking of ourselves as lie detectors and start thinking of ourselves as information gatherers."

She divides the room into pairs for a simulated interview. One plays the officer, the other the suspect. The scenario: a missing laptop, a teenage suspect, conflicting witness statements.

In the "old school" role-play, the officer leans in, ramps up the volume, and deploys the classic: "We know you did it, so you might as well tell the truth." The suspect crumbles, offering a stilted, barely plausible confession. The rest of the class watches, arms folded, familiar with the script.

Then, the instructor runs the exercise again—but this time, using the new curriculum.

"Start by building rapport," she instructs. "Don't accuse. Ask open-ended questions. Listen for what isn't said."

The difference is immediate. The officer opens with a question about the suspect's day. She asks about the friends, the classes, the schedule. The suspect, caught off guard by the lack of pressure, admits to borrowing the laptop but insists she meant to return it.

The instructor pauses the simulation. "Notice: No confession, but also no escalation. We learn more this way. And if there was a crime? The evidence is more reliable."

A slide appears on the board: "AVOIDING FALSE CONFESSIONS—TOP FIVE MODULES." The instructor walks the class through each:

1. **Distinguishing Interview vs. Interrogation**: Most mistakes happen because officers shift too early from information-gathering to accusation. The new protocol delays confrontation until corroborating evidence exists. The difference is not just semantic; it's strategic.

2. **Recognizing Signs of Cognitive Disability or Mental Illness**: Every recruit now learns to spot red flags: flat affect, confusion with time and sequence, hypercompliance. The policy is clear: If a suspect seems lost, the interview pauses for assessment. Sometimes, a clinician joins. Sometimes, the session ends.

3. **Avoiding Leading Questions**: Instructors drill this relentlessly. “Instead of ‘You did it, didn’t you?’ try ‘Tell me what happened from your point of view.’” Officers are taught to flag their own language in real time, or to tag and review recordings afterward.

4. **Understanding Memory’s Limits**: Officers watch testimony from memory experts, see how easily a narrative can be shaped by repeated suggestion. They learn to spot when a story has drifted—when a suspect’s “maybe” has been coaxed into a “definitely.”

5. **Mitigating Contamination from Prior Evidence**: Before each interview, officers sign a checklist confirming they have not reviewed uncorroborated witness statements, rumors, or social media posts. The process is structured to minimize “leakage”—the subtle feeding of facts that a suspect could not know.

As the modules tick by, the mood in the room changes. At first, there is skepticism—old hands mumbling about “softer policing,” jokes about needing a degree just to ask a question. But then, the instructor pulls up a case study: A wrongful conviction overturned after seventeen years because an intellectually disabled man “confessed” to a crime he did not understand.

She plays two minutes of the original interrogation tape, then two minutes of a post-reform simulation with a matched subject. The difference is humiliating. In the first, the officer bulldozes every hesitation, ending each question with, "That's right, isn't it?" In the second, the interviewer repeats the Miranda warning, slows the pace, and checks in after every answer. The "suspect" never confesses, but he does point investigators toward the true perpetrator.

A detective in the back—older, mustached, rumored to have seen it all—raises his hand. "So you're saying everything we learned was wrong?"

The instructor answers without missing a beat. "Not wrong. Just incomplete. We're not perfect. The job is to get better."

The next slide is a map, showing before-and-after false confession rates in departments that adopted the new training. In the pilot cities—Seattle, Chicago, Boston—the rate dropped by a quarter, then by a third. In New Jersey, the first state to mandate advanced interview training for all detectives, the drop was nearly fifty percent.

Below the chart, a line from a peer-reviewed study is highlighted:

"Properly trained officers elicit the same number of confessions, but the proportion of true confessions increases, and wrongful admissions decrease dramatically."

The instructor opens the floor to discussion. At first, the comments are cautious. "It'll take longer to close a case," one officer says. Another: "Suspects will game the system, lawyer up." But a younger patrolman, barely out of probation, says: "If it means fewer bad busts, I'm for it."

She pulls up quotes from officers in post-reform departments:

- "At first, it felt like the training slowed me down. Now, I don't lose sleep over whether I got it right."

- "The first time I spotted a suspect with an undiagnosed mental disability, I paused and called in a supervisor. We didn't get a confession, but it turned out he was innocent."

- "When we switched from aggressive tactics to open-ended interviews, our clearance rate stayed the same. The difference is, nobody is coming back years later saying we railroaded them."

The session closes with a mock trial: officers take turns testifying in court, with a local defense attorney playing cross-examiner. Every leading question, every lapse in protocol, is called out and debated. The point is not to catch mistakes, but to normalize the idea that scrutiny is part of the job.

In the hallway, as the group files out, two detectives linger. One says, "You think they're ever going to stop second-guessing us?" The other, a little less defensive, says, "Maybe if we get it right the first time, they won't have to."

The new script is clear: The best confession is the one that survives sunlight. Training is no longer about closing a case. It is about making the truth so sturdy that even years, or decades, cannot undo it.

In the months after the training, the department's internal audit reports its first year with zero sustained complaints of coercion or misconduct. Clearance rates hold. Court backlogs shrink, as fewer confessions are challenged and fewer cases are thrown out.

For the officers, the change is more subtle. Some miss the adrenaline of the old ways. Others welcome the relief: No more 2 a.m. phone calls from Internal Affairs, no more depositions, no more sense of being the villain in someone else's story.

For the system, the benefit is undeniable. Each avoided error saves not only millions in settlements and retrials, but something harder to quantify: The trust that the next confession will be real.

The ticking clock is the most reliable witness in any interrogation room. For decades, its testimony was ignored. Hours ticked by, day dissolved into night, and the subject—once sharp, then sullen, then desperate—sat as the clock counted down their resistance.

It took the better part of a century for science to catch up. In the early 2000s, a team at Northwestern University ran the numbers: the average time to confession, in both true and false cases, was under three hours. But the average length of a false confession session? More than twice that. For every additional hour, the likelihood of a suspect saying what the interrogator wanted jumped—especially if the suspect was young, sleep-deprived, or in withdrawal.

A law review article put it bluntly: "The function of prolonged interrogation is not to extract truth, but to exhaust alternatives."

The research made headlines. But change, as always, came slow. In some jurisdictions, the idea of limiting an interrogation to "just" four or six hours was viewed as surrender—a concession to criminality, a bureaucratic handcuff on honest police work. Yet the data piled up: In cities where time limits were piloted, false confession rates dropped by up to 40%. Clearance rates held steady, and—in a twist that rankled the old guard—case closure times actually improved. Investigators, forced to prepare, entered the room with a plan, not a script.

The protocol in these places reads like an airline checklist:

- No continuous session longer than four hours.

- Mandatory breaks for food, water, and restroom use.

- If the subject is a minor or flagged as vulnerable, a break every two hours—no exceptions.

- After the maximum time, the interview is paused and subject is offered the option of counsel.

For the typical detective, this is a culture shock. The marathon sessions—the slow boiling of the suspect—are gone. In their place is a series of sprints, each with a defined goal. "It's like playing chess on a clock," one officer says. "You have to use every minute wisely."

In practice, the results are unambiguous. Consider the case of "J.T.," a high school senior suspected of arson in his own neighborhood. The old model would have kept him in the box from dusk till dawn, cycling through "good cop," "bad cop," and every flavor in between. Under the new rules, his session lasts just under three hours, with a ten-minute break at the halfway point for a sandwich and a soda. He never confesses, but does point police to a friend who borrowed his lighter. The friend, when brought in, is offered the same schedule. Within two sessions, the real arsonist is identified and the case closed, all without a single claim of coercion.

Compare this to a headline from the last decade: "Teen Admits Guilt After 18 Hours, Later Exonerated by DNA." The difference is not subtle.

The logic behind the reform is borrowed from labor law. No one expects a surgeon or airline pilot to operate at peak after ten straight hours. Why should we expect the most critical fact-finding in the justice system to happen when everyone is least alert, most desperate?

The next layer of reform is legal: mandatory presence of counsel for vulnerable suspects. The term "vulnerable" is defined broadly—anyone under eighteen, anyone flagged for cognitive impairment, anyone with limited English proficiency. In the reform states, the moment a box is checked on the intake form, the interview cannot begin until counsel is present.

Critics predicted this would stonewall all questioning, clog the courts with "lawyering up." But the effect was subtler. In Cook County, where the reform rolled out ahead of the rest, the volume of confessions dipped at first, but then rebounded. The difference was the content: confessions became shorter, less rambling, more factually consistent. And, crucially, the number of retracted or disputed confessions—already a litigation nightmare—fell almost to zero.

In the new paradigm, the attorney is not a silent fixture but an active participant. In some rooms, they sit beside the suspect and signal when a question is unclear or inappropriate. In others, they are a virtual presence—a tablet propped on the table, the lawyer's face hovering in the corner of the frame like a modern Jiminy Cricket.

A case study: a fourteen-year-old brought in for questioning about a stolen bicycle. The lawyer, called in from a pro bono list, arrives within an hour. She requests a break every forty-five minutes, gently redirects questions that verge on leading, and twice reminds the officers to clarify the right to silence. In the end, the boy admits to watching the theft, not to committing it. His story matches video evidence, and the real thief is caught the next week. There are no appeals, no lawsuits, no years of simmering injustice.

In another: A man with mild intellectual disability is accused of petty theft from his workplace. In the old days, he would have crumbled in minutes, agreeing to any narrative that ended the session. Now, with counsel present, he holds his ground. The questioning is direct but not repetitive. After a short break, the employer's inventory records are reviewed—and show the items were never missing in the first place.

The statistics are impressive, but the change in tone is harder to measure. In community forums, parents and advocates no longer recount horror stories of children "confessing" to things they couldn't have known. Public defenders, once resigned to cleaning up the messes of interrogation, now arrive at arraignment to find their clients' statements clear and uncontested.

The clock is no longer a weapon, but a witness. And, for the first time, it testifies equally for both sides.

For most of the twentieth century, the gold standard for interrogation was "get the confession, by any means short of a bruise." The methods were as much folklore as science—good cop/bad cop, rapid-fire accusation, baiting the subject with lies about evidence, threatening lengthy sentences or dangling the hope of leniency. The idea was not to uncover the truth, but to elicit an admission that would hold up in court.

The aftermath of the DNA revolution detonated this paradigm. Suddenly, hundreds of cases with "airtight" confessions fell apart when a hair or a swab proved the suspect's innocence. Old methods—once legendary, even mythologized in detective circles—were revealed to be not just unreliable, but actively hazardous to justice.

The new wave of reform did not originate in the U.S. It came, like many public safety innovations, from the UK. There, in the wake of several infamous miscarriage-of-justice cases, the Home Office commissioned a wholesale redesign of the investigative interview. The result: the PEACE model.

PEACE is not an acronym built for branding, but for process:

- **Planning and Preparation**

- **Engage and Explain**

- **Account**

- **Closure**

- **Evaluate**

It is an architecture of patience. The emphasis is on information, not confession; on the careful, methodical construction of a narrative, not the quick win.

In the new training modules, officers learn to spend as much time preparing for an interview as they do conducting it. They review case facts, hypothesize plausible scenarios, and set concrete goals: What do I want to learn? What are my blind spots? Am I walking in already convinced of what happened?

The next step, Engage and Explain, is all about building rapport—not as a manipulation, but as a genuine attempt to reduce anxiety. Officers introduce themselves by first name, outline the process, and ask the subject if they understand. No games, no tricks.

The Account phase is the heart of the interview. Here, the subject tells their story, start to finish, uninterrupted. The interviewer listens—really listens—pausing only to clarify points or mark times for later follow-up. No leading questions, no loaded phrasing. Once the narrative is laid out, the interviewer circles back, asking for details, gently highlighting contradictions, but always letting the subject do the work of narrating.

Closure is exactly what it sounds like: The session ends with a recap, an opportunity for the subject to correct or add to their story. The interviewer explains next steps, thanks the subject for their time, and ends the session with a clear signal that they are leaving the room as equals.

Evaluate comes last. The officer reviews the interview, alone or with a supervisor. They ask: Did I learn what I needed to learn? Did I introduce bias? Were there points where I lost neutrality? It is a built-in mechanism for self-correction—a system that assumes fallibility, then designs around it.

The difference between PEACE and its predecessors is as stark as analog and digital.

In field tests, departments using the PEACE model saw a reduction in both overall confessions and, more importantly, in false confessions. The cases that did go forward were cleaner, less vulnerable to appeal, and more likely to survive scrutiny from judges and juries trained to spot psychological coercion.

One internal review in London compared two homicide squads, one using the PEACE model, one the legacy approach. The PEACE squad closed slightly fewer cases with confessions—but the cases that went to court had a 20% higher conviction rate. And, for the first time in decades, not a single false confession was overturned in appellate court.

Back in the States, early adopters of the model found similar results. In a suburb of Minneapolis, the police department reported that after two years of PEACE-based interviewing, none of their cases had been challenged for coercion or contamination. The public defenders' office, once the most strident critics of police practice, began recommending the local force as a "model for humane and effective investigation." Crime rates did not spike. Case clearance did not collapse. The only thing missing was the familiar churn of lawsuits and botched convictions.

The transition is not always smooth. In some precincts, the old guard bristles at the "softness" of the new technique. They argue that criminals will walk, that the absence of pressure equals impunity. But in the rooms where the PEACE model is practiced faithfully, the dynamic changes. Suspects, no longer on guard for a trap, volunteer details they might otherwise withhold. Officers, less invested in a specific outcome, are more likely to catch lies—and, just as crucially, to recognize when the subject is telling the truth.

The role of DNA exonerations in driving this change cannot be overstated. In the decades after the first Innocence Project case, more than 350 people in the U.S. were freed after DNA proved their innocence. In nearly one-quarter of these cases, a false confession was central to the conviction. For years, each exoneration was met with a round of finger-pointing: Was it the detective's fault? The suspect's suggestibility? The DA's tunnel vision? The answer, of course, was all of the above.

But the real power of DNA was not in exonerating individuals. It was in showing, beyond reasonable doubt, that the problem was systemic. The same mistakes kept happening, county to county, state to state. Once the numbers became impossible to ignore, the conversation shifted. No longer could a single department claim "one bad apple." The apples, it seemed, were everywhere, and so the orchard had to change.

The numbers tell the story. In 1990, the first year DNA was used in criminal court, the national exoneration database recorded fewer than ten overturned cases. By 2010, the number was in the hundreds. Each new case was an indictment not just of the conviction, but of the entire investigative culture that made it possible.

Reformers seized the momentum. Advocacy groups lobbied legislatures to fund PEACE training. Law schools rewrote their criminal procedure courses to include modules on cognitive bias and confession contamination. Judges began instructing juries to treat "admissions against interest" with the same skepticism reserved for eyewitness ID.

It is not a clean or complete revolution—many precincts still cling to the old methods, and the appeal of a "slam-dunk" confession will never fully disappear. But the trajectory is clear. Every year, more departments make the switch. Every year, the rate of DNA-proven false confession cases drops a little more.

Consider a scene from a reformed room:

The suspect, a twenty-year-old college student, is brought in for questioning about a robbery. The officer—first name only, no visible weapon—sits across, tablet open.

"Do you understand why you're here?" she asks.

The student nods.

"Can you tell me, in your own words, what you were doing last night?"

The story is halting, but consistent. The officer listens, asks about timing, clarifies a gap. When the narrative is finished, she asks, "Is there anything else you want to add?" The student shakes his head.

A day later, video from a nearby ATM corroborates the student's story. No further interview is needed. The case is closed, the subject goes home.

No confession is wrung out of thin air. No script is forced into the record. Just the facts, as best as anyone can state them.

This is the legacy of the DNA era: Not just justice for the wrongly accused, but a blueprint for never making the same mistake again.

Every movement needs its engine, and in the fight to reform interrogation, advocacy groups are the spark and the fuel. The best-known, the Innocence Project, operates from a suite of cubicles in lower Manhattan—a space more crowded startup than marble nonprofit. The walls are lined with photos of exonerees, each smiling awkwardly, some clutching the hands of family, others holding up a court order like a lottery ticket.

The mood is intense, caffeinated, and unapologetically adversarial. Phones ring. Interns hunch over spreadsheets, cross-referencing case law and forensic reports. At a round table, two attorneys run through a war game: which cases to prioritize for DNA review, which legislative hearings to target next, which judges might be swayed by the latest research. The mission is clear: get the innocent out, and change the rules so fewer end up in.

The playbook is as much PR as it is law. Every new exoneration is blasted out on social media, paired with data: "John Doe, freed after 26 years—confessed to a crime he didn't commit. See how time limits and mandatory video could have prevented this." There are hashtags, press releases, even a short documentary series on YouTube. Each case becomes a parable, a lesson aimed not at the converted but at the voting public and the policymakers whose inboxes overflow with constituent outrage.

The results are tangible. In a single year, advocates helped pass laws mandating video recording of interrogations in four states. In two others, they forced the adoption of the PEACE model by threatening class-action lawsuits. Lobbyists, some ex-prosecutors, some ex-defenders, shuttle between capitols with binders of horror stories and bar charts showing the savings—money, years, trust—when wrongful convictions are reduced.

The ripple effects are everywhere. At police conferences, officers who once dismissed the Innocence Project as a nuisance now invite staff to run training sessions. At universities, law schools add seminars on interrogation ethics to their core curriculum. In court, judges increasingly cite amicus briefs from advocacy groups when issuing decisions on suppression or admissibility.

But the real battle is at the level of process. The advocates know they can't fix every case, but they can rewrite the operating system that produces the cases. And so, in legislative subcommittees and blue-ribbon commissions, they lobby for a package of reforms—a practical framework for ending the era of the weaponized confession.

The framework is modular, adaptable for every jurisdiction, but the essentials are always the same:

1. Universal Recording: Every word, from first hello to last signature, on audio and video. No more "he said/she said." No more selective memory. The tape is the record.

2. Evidence-Based Interrogation: Out with the Reid technique, in with PEACE or its local equivalent. Officers are required to train and re-certify, with ongoing evaluation for compliance.

3. Time Limits and Breaks: Maximum session times, enforced by policy and monitored by supervisors. Rest, food, and bathroom breaks as a matter of right, not privilege.

4. Mandatory Counsel for Vulnerable Suspects: Underage? Cognitive disability? Not fluent in English? No interview without a lawyer present.

5. Disincentives for Bad Faith: If a court finds coercion or contamination, not only is the confession tossed, but the officer is flagged for review—and, if necessary, discipline.

6. Independent Case Review: Every serious conviction is subject to a post-judgment audit, especially if new forensic evidence emerges. Oversight is external; no more letting police police themselves.

7. Transparency and Community Oversight: Departments publish anonymized data on confessions, complaints, and exonerations. Civilian boards have standing to review practices and recommend policy changes.

For each step, there is a script—a model bill, a checklist, a training module. The advocates email these to statehouses, city councils, and police unions, ready to deploy at the first sign of political will.

But reform is not just policy; it is culture. And changing culture is slow, granular work. The Innocence Project and its siblings do this, too: running school workshops, partnering with churches and mosques, showing up at every community forum where a parent or a pastor wants to know why the police are still "putting words in kids' mouths." They train a generation of volunteers to spot warning signs and intervene early.

In the courts, the effects trickle upward. Prosecutors, once the most relentless confession-seekers, now vet every statement for "contamination risk." They toss out shaky confessions preemptively, knowing the odds of reversal have gone up. Public defenders demand the full video, and when it's missing or incomplete, they move for dismissal. Judges, too, are less likely to treat confession as gospel; jury instructions now include specific warnings about the unreliability of admissions under pressure.

At the national level, lawmakers convene "truth and reconciliation" hearings—not just to catalogue the wrongs of the past, but to set the rules for the future. Experts testify. Exonerees testify. Sometimes, even the officers who once took the confessions testify, confessing to their own mistakes.

Each reform is a stitch in the fabric of a new system. But the work is never finished.

A week after a new law goes into effect in Michigan, the advocacy team watches the local news as a city councilmember brags about "ending the dark era of coercion." In the office, a volunteer puts a gold star next to the state on a giant map pinned to the wall. Then they turn back to the phones, because the inbox is still full of letters: My son confessed to something he didn't do. My brother has an intellectual disability and confessed just to go home. What can you do to help?

The roadmap for reform is everywhere now: in best-practice toolkits, in police academy syllabi, in court opinions and op-ed pages. The next challenge is scale.

The advocates know it is not enough to patch the system. The ultimate goal is to invert the metrics of success. Not "cases closed," but "cases closed justly." Not "confessions secured," but "truths established, beyond reasonable doubt."

To get there, each group—police, prosecutors, defenders, judges, legislators—has its action steps.

For police: Embrace the new training, record everything, report out the numbers.

For prosecutors: Audit cases, cross-check evidence, let go of the win-at-all-costs mentality.

For defenders: Demand transparency, teach clients their rights, flag every questionable confession.

For judges: Apply rigorous standards to confession admissibility; insist on best practice.

For lawmakers: Fund reform, create independent oversight, and keep the pressure on.

And for the public: Stay vigilant. Hold the system to account. Believe that progress is possible, but only if the demand for it never stops.

The new definition of justice is not just punishing the guilty. It is protecting the innocent, even—especially—when that means tearing up the rulebook.

In the plaza from the chapter's start, the engraved wall waits in the blue dusk. Some names are old, most are recent. But every year, the additions slow; the next generation's names, it is hoped, will never need to be carved in stone. Above the wall, the city's light glows brighter, just perceptibly, as the system learns—imperfectly, relentlessly—to bend toward truth.

About the Author

Brian Leslie is a coercive interrogation & interview techniques expert, with over 14 years of previous law enforcement experience which includes major case investigation and specialized training, as well as a term serving as Chief of Police. Mr. Leslie has testified and been qualified as an expert in Federal, State and Military Courts throughout the United States. You can contact Brian Leslie to consult on a case at 1-888-400-1309 or at brian@criminalcaseconsultants.com

Read more at https://www.brianlesliemedia.com.

TRUE
AMERICAN
PUBLISHING

About the Publisher

As a boutique book publisher, we take on only a few new authors per year. We focus on building an author's brand, thereby directing more resources towards their overall success. Authors accepted by True American Publishing become creative partners, therefore, participating in their own success.

www.ingramcontent.com/pod-product-compliance
Lightning Source LLC
LaVergne TN
LVHW090404210926
848480LV00002B/443
* 9 7 9 8 2 3 3 5 3 7 6 5 3 *